THE SUND

How to Run a Successful Conference

SECOND EDITION

John G Fisher

First published in 1998
Second edition published in 2000

Kogan Page Limited
120 Pentonville Road
London N1 9JN

British Library Cataloguing in Publication Data

A CIP record for this book is available from the British Library.

ISBN 0 7494 3406 6

Cover design by DW Design, London
Typeset by Jean Cussons Typesetting, Diss, Norfolk
Printed and bound in Great Britain by Clays Ltd, St Ives plc

contents

introduction

Many thousands, and possibly millions, of formal meetings are held every day across the world in conference centres, hotels and commercial venues. But despite the creeping influence of technology, which is making it less and less necessary for people to have to meet, the market is actually growing. More people than ever before are opting to meet up rather than exchange e-mails. As a consequence of this growth, more people lower down the organization are experiencing conferences, either arranged by their employer, by suppliers or by industry bodies. But we all know that familiarity can breed contempt. Conferences come in all shapes and sizes, and are of varying quality. Conferences are no longer a once a year, out-of-the-ordinary activity. That's why running them successfully has become an important goal of any organization wishing to get its message over effectively.

But success is only relative. For a conference to be successful, several factors need to be right:

- the objectives need to be clearly defined;
- the venue should be appropriate;
- communication should be creative but relevant;
- logistics need careful planning;
- accommodation and banqueting requires detailed input;
- budgets and cashflow have to be controlled.

These factors can be judged in two ways: by ensuring that the executive responsible for the event's management is aware of what makes a successful conference, and by listening to what delegates think, both before and after the event.

One of the most common errors in conference management is to assume that you can buy your way out of trouble. An extravagant creative theme or a big-name speaker may not be relevant for every type of conference. In fact, in most cases, they prove to be an expensive distraction. Post-event research usually reveals that the delegates remembered the famous celebrity but could not recall the main thrust of the conference message.

Equally, spending too little money results in delegates complaining about 'hygiene' factors (food, accommodation, temperature, poor presentation), and not taking to heart the core corporate messages.

The aim of this brief guide is to help anyone who has been given the task of running a conference, either as a one-off project or as an integral part of their sales, marketing or human resources role. It provides a running track for ensuring that essential issues are encountered in the right sequence. The result should be to create a relaxed working environment for the conference delegates, so that you, as conference organizer can concentrate on the inevitable unexpected issues which will need to be dealt with on the day itself.

The advent of ADSL communication links and video-conferencing (see Chapter 10) may well, in time, reduce the number of regular internal meetings an organization needs to arrange, but larger groups of people will continue to want to meet face-to-face on the wider issues. It is often said that 80 per cent of any corporate message comes from non-verbal cues. Walking the talk is as important as saying the right things. To communicate at the highest level of quality you need to be in the same room and in physical contact with fellow communicants, so that delegates can see as well as hear the message. That's what conferences are about – and will continue to be about for the foreseeable future.

to the reader

So, you've been given a conference to run. Whether it's part of your job or you are a complete novice, you will only get one chance to get it right. It is a 'live' event, which cannot be rerun. Your professional efficiency and perhaps even your standing in the organization will be under the most public scrutiny. Get it right and you will be surprised at the silence, albeit an admiring one. Get it wrong and you'll carry the memories with you for many years to come.

But don't panic – there really is no need. As with most organizational projects, there is a formula you can follow and a sequence you can go through to minimize the risk of failure. Nothing in this book should come as a surprise, whether you are a seasoned professional or a once-a-year organizer. The trick is to manage, in the right sequence, all those who contribute to the success of the conference, either by supplying services or by contributing as speakers. You need to be aware of the critical path which leads to success.

Perhaps the most difficult aspect is to keep everyone on track. This is particularly hard if you hold a relatively junior position in the organization but need the most senior people to play their part at the right time in your schedule.

This book will help you to schedule the process of organizing your conference in such a way that rank will not be a problem. Your preparation will be such that even the CEO will toe the line (well, perhaps not all the time – but enough for you to build in some contingency planning).

There is only one principle behind producing a successful conference: attention to detail. You need to be sceptical of any element that refuses to be pinned down. That goes for hotel staff and creative producers as well as your own internal speakers. You will probably be the only person in your entire organization who has all the detail. If someone decides to examine any aspect of it, you need the plan to be accurate. Many people, some of them senior professionals in their own right, will only be playing their part. Don't expect them, however senior, to appreciate all your problems. Only you know what everyone should be doing at any one time.

A perfect conference is when no one notices the logistics, and the delegates simply receive the organizational messages with ringing clarity. Your job, at the end of the day, is to keep your cool, while others may be losing theirs; and to deliver a professional event. The highest compliment you can receive is for people to say, 'Conference organizer? I didn't realize there was one!'

do you really need a conference?

It sounds self-defeating to start a book about conferences by questioning whether you really need one at all. But there is a serious point to consider. Is your conference absolutely necessary?

The decision to hold a conference is often made long before the conference organizer is involved, so in many instances the question of value for money will already have been debated and concluded. But a good conference organizer will still want reassurance that there is a good business case for the event and that it has everyone's full support. The last thing you want is people dragging their feet when you are relying on their cooperation to meet a deadline.

So, whether you were involved in the initial decision or not, you need to satisfy yourself that a conference is indeed the most effective way to achieve the organization's goals. What are the main reasons for wanting to hold a conference?

reasons for a conference

passing on information

Conferences provide a unique medium for putting information over. This is particularly important for new products and services, which require explanation or demonstration. A conference can also ensure that everyone is informed at the same time in the same controlled environment. This may be important if the subject matter is confidential or only applies to a specific level or type of delegate. A product launch or a press conference are good examples.

boosting morale

Questions about organizational morale can be tackled effectively in a conference setting, as distractions are kept to a minimum and senior management can be seen to be concerned and taking action. Live input using interactive technology can help to generate a level of debate which it is difficult to achieve on a piecemeal basis back in the office.

making internal announcements

Whether the news is of a corporate merger or new government legislation, one of the best ways to explain implications and reassure staff is to hold an internal conference. In such situations delegates will want to know how the changes will affect them on an individual basis, while still feeling that their managers are in control of the bigger picture.

communicating with the sales force

Every organization needs to sell its products and services, either overtly or in more subtle ways. A conference is an ideal way to communicate with salespeople, many of whom may work from home and have relatively little contact with the organization unless they are chasing product delivery promises or querying their pay cheques. A conference provides them with the opportunity to meet their peers, tackle real people with their administrative problems and focus their own activity behind the wider corporate goals.

facilitating trade and delivering training

Perhaps the most visible aspects of the conference industry to non-specialists are association meetings and training events. A conference is often the chosen means of enabling people from different parts of the country or the world to interact, and offering them a formal opportunity to put their views across.

reasons against a conference

But conferences can be expensive. Assuming the average number of delegates to be 50, you need to feed them, hire a presentation room, pay for staging and cover their overnight accommodation. You may have to provide drinks in the bar and even pay for their travel expenses. Large numbers and substantial budgets are commonplace in the automotive industry, for example, where a new car launch needs to be rolled-out to a variety of potential delegates including dealers, customers, and the media.

Could your initiative to communicate to a large number of people be handled more effectively using alternative media? There are a number of techniques you could choose from to disseminate information without needing to go to the expense and man-hours of running a conference.

alternative conference media

Advantages	Disadvantages
Video	
▦ Inexpensive for large numbers	▦ Can appear impersonal
▦ Quick lead time	▦ Not interactive
▦ Complete control of message	▦ Minimal detail
Brochure	
▦ Flexible distribution	▦ Requires detailed study
▦ Provides substantial detail	▦ May not suit all employees
▦ Permanent record	▦ Not interactive
e-mail	
▦ Quick	▦ Impersonal
▦ Good for detail	▦ Can be misinterpreted
▦ Simultaneous	▦ Too easy to ignore
Video-conferencing	
▦ Instant feedback	▦ Small numbers
▦ Relatively inexpensive	▦ Requires training in techniques
▦ Discussions possible	▦ Perceived as gimmicky
Distance learning	
▦ Full involvement	▦ Not interactive, normally
▦ Good on detail	▦ Requires briefing
▦ Measures learning level	▦ No 'group' feeling

As with all marketing techniques there is always a trade-off between set-up costs and run-on costs, depending on volume. Only you know which would be the more efficient way to achieve the organization's aims.

A simple checklist may be useful to help you help your organization decide whether a conference is the most preferred route.

conference need checklist

Marks out of 10

1. Large numbers (over 50)
2. Needs to be simultaneous/interactive
3. Quality presentation must reflect message
4. Information flow needs careful management
5. Must build morale

Total

A total score of less than 25 out of 50 might cause you to rethink whether a conference should be the chosen communication technique.

Research into the market tells us consistently that about a third of all conferences are small executive meetings, and another third are to do with training, the balance being split between sales/product launches, general management meetings and incentive conferences (the last of these accounting for only 4 per cent). So most conferences are fairly well-defined with specific parameters. The challenge is how to tackle those events on the fringes, which defy the application of a tried and tested formula. If this is your type of conference (a sales event, a product launch, a corporate merger, for example) you need to take great care that, having decided that a conference is indeed the chosen medium, you are crystal clear about what it is for. In other words, clarify your objectives.

setting objectives

Setting objectives may not be something you can do all by yourself, even though you may have been given the task of organizing the conference. Your job is to get the initiators to clarify for you their objectives for the event. This may not be an easy task. If you tackle it half-heartedly, you simply get platitudes. If you approach it too aggressively, you risk alienating the very people from whom you need cooperation (what's more, they are probably more senior than you, so being heavy-handed is not going to achieve a great deal).

The best way forward is to make an educated guess as to what the objectives may be, and then ask for comments and clarification. Here are some possible objectives for specific types of conference, which on the face of it may seem quite similar.

annual staff conference

- ▦ To present the current year results and next year's plan.
- ▦ To announce structural changes (merger, acquisition, staffing levels).
- ▦ To create a team-feeling.
- ▦ To obtain staff input regarding future plans.
- ▦ To gain agreement regarding future plans.

sales conference

- ▦ To motivate sellers to sell more.
- ▦ To reward sellers for their achievement.
- ▦ To launch a new incentive programme.
- ▦ To explain a new sales contract.
- ▦ To launch a new product/new annual targets.

management conference

- ▦ To announce future plans to management.
- ▦ To obtain input from management about future plans.
- ▦ To create future plans for the organization.

▓ To pre-launch initiatives to the management team.
▓ To improve morale among the management team.

trade or technical conference

▓ To demonstrate specific products and services.
▓ To provide a forum for gathering industry knowledge.
▓ To teach delegates specific industry skills.
▓ To respond to social or legislative issues.
▓ To provide contact opportunities for specific buyers/ sellers.

distributor/network conference

▓ To motivate distributors to sell more of your product.
▓ To improve relationships with distributors.
▓ To gather new distributors.
▓ To announce administrative changes.
▓ To reward leading distributors.

It is clear from a brief glance at these five types of conference that each one may well have more than one objective. You will have already perceived that the style of each type of conference could be markedly different depending on the relationship between the sponsor (the organization which pays for the conference) and the delegate (the one who attends the conference). In some instances the organizer's view of what should be presented will be more affected by whether the delegates are required to pay to attend. Another important factor to bear in mind is whether attendance is obligatory (as in the case of a management conference). Each event will be subtly different in both tone and style, even though the objectives may be the same.

agreement on the main objective

So, once you have narrowed your objectives down to two or three, do all you can to get agreement on the one which, if all else fails, is the most important. Your conference will ultimately be judged on its achievement of the main objective. To avoid any potential recriminations or backsliding after the event, when all the costs start coming in, you need to be able to point to successful achievement of the main objective, as agreed by the senior management team. It may seem somewhat academic to be setting written objectives, but as your conference project progresses, you will be surprised at the number of times you refer back to your clearly defined objectives to help you accept or reject a new idea for a speaker or an embellishment to the conference arrangements.

Here are some objectives taken from a real conference for the senior management team of a global soft drinks company. The delegates were managing directors from over 70 locations around the world meeting to discuss forward strategy for the group.

conference objectives

- To debate future strategy.
- To encourage delegates to get to know each other on a first-name basis.
- To agree the general direction of the group.
- To have an enjoyable, memorable experience.

Each of these objectives was subsequently measured through post-event delegate research to provide a measure of success for the conference.

You need to be careful not to have too many objectives, or delegates and speakers may be confused as to the purpose of the conference. You also need to ensure you do not agree to run with conflicting objectives. There may well be situations where the CEO's objective is to inform about future strategy, but where the rest of the board want some direct input. Such discrepancies of focus can create considerable tension as the conference project progresses to the creative stage.

One technique to help isolate the main or overriding objective is to ask a simple questions: 'What do you want delegates to feel as they leave the conference?' This provokes a number of responses, depending on the point of view or functional responsibility of the person being questioned. But it helps to strip away any vagueness and often produces an overriding objective with which everyone can agree.

examples of main objectives

- ▨ 'We want everyone to feel reassured.'
- ▨ 'We want them to know all about the new products.'
- ▨ 'We want them to be fired up about the incentive scheme.'
- ▨ 'We want to instil loyalty and commitment.'
- ▨ 'We want to explore the implications of the merger.'

Once everyone agrees on the main objective, you can add related, supporting objectives to provide even better focus for the content of the conference. If the main objective is to reassure staff, this could be supported by secondary objectives such as providing an opportunity for delegate input, explaining in detail the new organizational structure and creating opportunities for staff to talk about the issues with key managers (perhaps through hosted tables at the luncheon or through break-out sessions).

In this way, all those who have an input to the conference are committed to a united view of its purpose. This agreement will be of enormous value as you move into the organizational phase of managing the conference. Every professional organizer will tell you that it is time well spent.

measuring your objectives

A further refinement could be to quantify those objectives, if at all possible. There may be company-wide surveys that regularly measure morale, on which you can piggyback. By asking specific questions about the conference and the corporate mood afterwards, you can get an indication of the effectiveness of your event.

Those who organize conferences on a regular basis tend to have a rolling measure of effectiveness, which they update each time they run an event. Questions about the appropriateness of the venue, the programme content, the banqueting and the travel arrangements, are routinely monitored to ensure the best possible use of resources. It is always useful to be able to defend against isolated criticism by being able to quote the considered opinions of the majority.

One additional benefit of gathering statistical information in this way is its usefulness in planning future events. One of the first places to look when devising the shape and format of a future conference is at the research of the last event. If 89 per cent of delegates found the day's content 'uninformative', you know what you need to concentrate on to make the next event better. More about this in Chapter 9 '(('What went right, what went wrong').

special announcements

The final aspect to check, before launching yourself into the mass of detailed organizing, is whether there are any special developments or announcements in the organizational pipeline which could alter your plan.

Typically, this could be a new product or service whose development schedule may not be as robust as your own. It is not uncommon for a manufacturing business to encounter unexpected production problems in the run-up to a launch, and have to postpone the announcement. If details of the new product are not central to the rationale for the conference, you can set up a contingency session for that element of your event. But if it is the main reason for meeting, you need to ensure that everyone is aware of the cost implications of cancelling the conference before you commit your organization to supplier contracts – or even the loss of face if you have no new product to demonstrate. More confidential issues, such as corporate mergers or changes in structure, are often subject to last-minute alteration or sometimes cancellation. Make sure you are at least aware of the potential need to postpone, even if you cannot be told the detail, so that you can act accordingly.

By now you will have reassured yourself that there is a good business case for the conference, and that there is agreement about the main objective and any subsidiary objectives. You will also have checked there are no 'bigger issues' which could cause your event to be cancelled.

Now you can start to think about the budget.

your conference checklist

- ▓ Clarify business rationale for conference. ☐
- ▓ Clarify type of conference. ☐
- ▓ Agree main objective. ☐
- ▓ Agree supporting objectives. ☐
- ▓ Check 'big issue' risk. ☐

building the budget

Defining the budget is your first big challenge as a conference organizer. If you are organizing an internal staff or distributor conference, senior management may well have handed you a budget to work with. An experienced organizer will know whether the budget is sufficient to do the job to the standard expected. But if you are running a conference for the first time, or perhaps having to organize a particular type of conference for the first time, how do you know what the budget should be? You don't, of course, until you add up the cost of everything you might need. So the response to being handed down a budget from on high is to say, 'Thank you very much, but let's talk through the brief first before we agree that there are sufficient funds to deliver the event you want'.

compile a wish list

As with all budgets you will have a list of fixed costs, which need to be covered regardless of the number of delegates. For conferences, the broad areas are staging and production costs, the invitation process, function room deposits, logistics and support fees. Variable costs cover the rest because the number of delegates drives almost every variable cost. The number of attendees is therefore vital to know (or estimate) before you can arrive at a working budget. A third, unwritten but inevitable cost is a contingency budget to cover additional drinks, production crew overtime, additional catering and unforeseen logistical costs, which will need to be covered as and when they arise because they are often beyond your control. It is impossible to be absolutely accurate about variable and contingency costs. Conferences are dynamic events with ever-changing emphases – even more so the closer you get to conference day. But you can make your life easier as the organizer by creating a workable budget in the early stages, otherwise you will spend all your energy robbing Peter to pay Paul, instead of concentrating on delivering the best conference your organization has ever had.

the fixed costs checklist

Production, speakers and staging are some of the biggest fixed cost elements of a conference, so you need to be aware of the major headings in each area.

All production costs should be viewed as fixed costs, even though within the production budget there is likely to be a good degree of movement as creative approaches change and ideas are added or removed. In terms of headings, you need to be aware of the following aspects.

projection

Costs include: screens, video projectors, slide projectors, video players (back-up player), preview monitor, interface unit, switcher, lectern monitors, scan converter, laser pointer, cabling, adaptors, prompting, lasers, video module creation fees, copies for distribution, live-links.

sound

Costs include: speakers, lectern microphones, tie-microphones, hand-held microphones, CD player, multicore, talkback system, mixer, q-lite system, cabling, adaptors, music copyright or creation fees.

speaker support

Costs include: design, image production – either 35mm slides or electronic images; based on average time taken, assume 150 images for a standard six-hour business conference. Additional costs for complicated, animated images, print proofs, script writing, speaker training, rehearsals on-site or off-site, flip charts, pens, peripherals.

staging

Costs include: design, lecterns, dais, backdrop, steps, furnishings, graphics, carpeting, seating area, special construction, drop banners, room decoration (duplicate set for roadshow), floor plans, revised layout plans.

lighting

Costs include: design, equipment hire, installation, crew, freight and transportation, rigging and de-rigging costs.

crew

Costs include: get-in crew, on-site crew, de-rigging crew, transportation, per diems (allowance for sustenance) for each crew member, show caller, script assistant, live video crew, lighting director/manager, sound technician, vision technician.

fees and insurances

Costs include: producer's fee, project fee, contingency for administration costs (3 per cent or whatever is agreed), equipment insurance.

Not every event will incur all these costs, but the golden rule is to establish a fixed budget once the creative response has been agreed. Any overspend will need to come from somewhere. It is better to confine the bargaining to within the production element, otherwise you may find yourself stinting on the gala dinner to cover the overspend on staging or equipment hire.

invitation process

Whether your invitation is a piece of direct mail, or a brochure, whether it involves checking the accuracy of a database list of invitees or making a series of telephone calls, the design and set-up costs will be a once-only expense, regardless of how many people attend the event. You should also include in your budget the costs of any advertising, posters or follow-up activity to boost delegate response as you approach the various contractual deadlines.

function rooms and contracts

Function room deposits will be payable if you want to secure specific rooms – 10 per cent is usually enough to show that you are serious, but for popular venues you may be asked to pay more. In addition, there is often a sliding scale of payments to be made as you approach the event. The venue will normally send you a contract to sign based on specific rooms, dates and projected numbers of delegates. The contract will show cancellation charges for downgrading of delegate numbers, so you need to be sure at the outset, within say 20 per cent, what your numbers will be. Although in theory, at least, many venue contracts go way over the top in protecting themselves against last-minute changes, in practice this is only to deter clients who habitually run two venues side by side to reduce their risk in case of low numbers. If you have been honest with the venue staff about your expectations, and kept them informed, few will hold you rigidly to the contract.

The one exception is cruise ships. They generally have somewhat one-sided contracts for charter which are so broad that one well-known ship owner even stipulates that the charter fee is still payable if the ship sinks before you get on board. Ship charters are one area where the lawyers definitely should be involved. Cruise ships aside, if you come a real cropper and for some unforeseen reason your conference cannot go ahead, you may be able to transfer the booking at the same venue to some future dates, at no charge. But do not count on it. When capacity in venues is running at between 85 per cent and 95 per cent, no venue owner wants to be left with empty rooms.

If there is something specific in the venue contract you cannot agree to, such as obligatory service payments or non-exclusivity of the venue, strike it out and sign the contract. The venue will always come back to you if they do not agree. One final element to bear in mind is what is excluded. With conference centres, you may well find all sorts of items which are charged obligatorily on consumption but which would not be charged by a hotel – such as security, electricity, water, the hire of chairs, signage, parking attendants and cloakroom staffing, to name but a few! If you are used to using hotels for conferences, pay particular attention when comparing per delegate headline rates from conference centres. At first glance conference centres look good value in comparison with hotels. But when all the bills finally come in, you will invariably find the conference centre option more expensive than the hotel. As the buyer, you need to make sure you really need all those conference centre frills before signing on the dotted line. Better still, do a budget based on a comparable local hotel and bargain your way to a better deal. There's nothing like competition, local or national, to get a venue to sharpen its pencil.

logistics and support fees

If part of your plan is to use an outside agency to help with registration or logistics, this cost will normally not change much from confirmation to completion, if the delegate numbers vary by less than 25 per cent. Assuming a rule of thumb of one agency person per 50 delegates (one per busload), you would need to miscalculate quite seriously to be able to reduce logistics costs once the agency has been appointed. But do think through when the support will actually be required. If the bulk of the extra work is for registration, there is no need to hang on doggedly to those staff all day. Contract them for four hours and save yourself half a day's rate.

set-up services

Set-up services include: security personnel, car parking attendants, signage, secretarial services and any other ancillary costs, which largely stand alone regardless of the number of delegates. All these costs mount up and can add as much as 10 per cent to the entire budget if you keep on saying 'Yes' every time they are offered. Always ask exactly what is planned, how long the service will be available, what the manpower will be and how the supplier can guarantee they will do a good job. Once you start to query these so-called extra services you may well find that they are unnecessary – so unless the venue puts them in the contract, do not feel obliged to take them on board.

Other one-off costs could include the provision of interpreters, initial recce costs, conference office costs, wet weather contingency, late bar staff, late bar licence. Do an exhaustive checklist so that you can cover everything. No event is ever exactly the same as any other, but in general your fixed costs are usually about 35 per cent of your total costs, although much depends on the nature of your contract with the chosen venue.

the variable costs checklist

The variable costs are usually the bulk of your budget, so these items need to be checked carefully if the budget is not to run away with itself. If there is any significant variance at the outset regarding the estimated number of delegates (as there may well be with third-party distributors or a paid-for conference), get agreement for a variable overall budget range. The worst organizational nightmare is trying to squeeze 500 delegates into an event designed and originally budgeted for 300 delegates. The CEO may be delighted at the event – but will be less so when you announce the 'unapproved' overspend of the total budget.

Variable costs can include:

▓ banqueting – food and drink.
▓ accommodation.
▓ travel.
▓ delegate print, menus, table plans.
▓ flowers on tables.
▓ table and room gifts.
▓ tips/service.
▓ porterage.
▓ parking, if applicable.
▓ insurances.
▓ purchase tax, if applicable.
▓ partner programme.

Unless you are running a regular event with good analysis of historic cost patterns, try to avoid the temptation to 'spend' any apparent extra funds which may be accruing as a result of lower-than-expected numbers of confirmed delegates. Most conference delegates leave it very late from a planning viewpoint to confirm their attendance, which often leads to a rush to register in the last two weeks – by which time you may have spent their variable cost allocation on fixed cost elements. How do you deal with finding cash for last minute, unforeseen expenses? Have a contingency budget.

contingency budget

Always build in at least 15 per cent as a contingency budget to cope with the unexpected. It is almost inevitable that something will crop up which draws on the contingency budget. Print items may need to be reprinted or couriered to the venue at the last minute. The CEO may insist on a better class of wine at the gala dinner. The on-site telephone bill is often more costly than expected, and you may have to find cash to persuade a freelance production crew to work through the night changing images or re-organizing the stage area. If you do not spend it because you are so well organized or have a particularly undemanding sponsor, you may come in under budget, and surprise your financial department and probably yourself.

The budget allocation table shows how you might expect your budget to be apportioned. If practical, use this model on a spreadsheet so you can alter the total budget if delegate numbers change or fixed cost items change. It is always useful in review meetings to be able to highlight the effect of adding items to, or subtracting them from, the overall budget. If you do not keep to this discipline, you may well find incremental costs creeping up, leaving you as a budget holder to carry the can once the show is over. For example, the sales department's whim to serve a glass of champagne to everyone at the gala dinner will have a knock-on effect on service, purchase tax, and

budget allocations

Table 2.1 Typical budget allocation

Fixed costs	Likely percentage
1. Production, staging and outside speakers	
2. Invitation process, marketing, design	
3. Conference rooms	
4. Agency fees, initial recce	
5. Signage	
6. Security, car parking set-up	35%
7. Cabaret, entertainment	
8. Registration costs	
9. Conference office costs, telephones, faxes	
10. Wet weather back-up, if applicable	

(Item 1 could be as much as 25% of total costs)

Variable costs (per delegate)	
1. Meals, breaks	
2. Drinks at meals, breaks	
3. Accommodation	
4. Travel	
5. Delegate print	
6. Table/room gifts	50%
7. Porterage, car parking per delegate	
8. Partner programme	
9. Late bar drinks	
10. Insurance, purchase tax	

Contingency	
1. 10% to cover all contingencies for direct costs	15%
2. Allowance for currency movements (if abroad)	

Total budget	**100%**

agency handling fees, in addition to the considerably marked-up cost of providing the champagne itself.

establish control at an early stage

In broad terms you may be overseeing 40 or more separate cost headings when you embark on planning a conference. By splitting the headings into fixed, variable and contingency categories, you will be able to establish budgetary control at an early stage. This is even more important if it is a commercial conference where your set-up costs are at risk until the day of the conference. By establishing control of costs at an early stage and being able to say what you are committed to in cost terms in the run-up to the big day, you can make sensible judgements as to whether to enhance the event or cut back, as appropriate.

your conference checklist

- ■ Compile your fixed costs list. ☐
- ■ Compile your variable costs list. ☐
- ■ Calculate a reasonable contingency. ☐
- ■ Review your costs regularly. ☐

finding the right venue

Once the objectives are crystal clear and the budget has been agreed at the highest possible level, you need to find a venue. Without a suitable venue, there will be no conference.

It sound obvious that this task needs to be completed first, but it is worth restating. Sometimes during the discussions about objectives, the debate will stray into choice of speakers, the creative approach, whether you should offer delegates an overnight stay and many other related issues. Much time can be lost at this stage while everyone is ignoring the most crucial factor: you need somewhere to hold the conference. As the conference organizer, you need now to be totally focused on finding the right venue. But no one should assume that you can simply book what you want when you want it, particularly during high season. For example, if the conference is for 500 people (not unusual) and you need overnight accommodation for them, there may only be a handful of options, unless you have had the foresight to book 12–18 months in advance.

matters of timing

A good place to start is the desired date-span. Your boss may have insisted in the brief to you that the conference must be on 14 April, but there are many reasons why being flexible and working hand-in-hand with the venues to find a convenient date can be mutually beneficial.

A knowledge of monthly hotel conference booking patterns may help, if the timing of your conference is not restricted to a particular month. The following list shows the percentage of conference bednights booked at a major hotel chain on a month-by-month basis:

July	7.3%
August	3.4%
September	9.8%
October	10.7%
November	10.8%
December	8.3%
January	7.6%
February	7.6%
March	8.9%
April	9.6%
May	7.4%
June	8.6%

The rank order of booking popularity per month is thus:

1. November.
2. October.
3. September.
4. April.
5. March.
6. June.
7. December.

8. January.
9. February.
10. May.
11. July.
12. August.

As you can see, August is the least popular month, while October and November are the most popular months. This pattern can vary from hotel to hotel. If it does not matter when your conference takes place, then July or August are excellent times because most hotels will offer extremely competitive rates to attract the business, particularly if overnight stays and banqueting are involved. However, because most people take holiday during this period, it is clearly not ideal from the delegates' point of view.

reporting cycles

Company reporting cycles also play a part when there is competition for venue space. An organization which has a January–December financial year will probably opt to convene in January to kick off the new year. An organization with an April–March financial year may well not be able to reveal results until May. November and early December tend to be particularly busy periods, as organizations tend to complete their budgeting cycle by this time and need to disseminate the following year's expenditure information before Christmas.

Often there are factors within the organization's industry sector which dictate the date-span. A substantial proportion of the toy industry's revenues is made in the six weeks leading up to Christmas. Conferences to present potential merchandise to retailers must therefore be held in June or July, to ensure their production lead times and promotional plans can be put in place for the festive retail season.

If your conference falls into one of the more normal categories outlined in Chapter 1, you will by definition be in competition with other organizations wanting the same dates.

A further date factor to recognize is the monthly cycle. Most meetings take place in the first 10 days of the month because, with budgets to achieve and sales targets to hit, the last week of the month is usually dedicated to key income-generating activity. This means that you may be able to negotiate a better price or find more available space towards the end of the month, due to there being marginally less demand.

day of the week

The day of the week also plays a part. Many buyers – either through bitter experience or pure prejudice – will insist on a Tuesday or a Wednesday. In general, Mondays and Fridays tend to be less popular for travel reasons. Sundays are virtually unheard-of for conferences. But this gives the wise conference organizer significant bargaining power, particularly if an overnight stay is involved. From a hotel perspective, Sunday night tends to be the least busy night of the week, so linking accommodation on Sunday night to a conference on Monday can be the basis of a very good deal. The same goes for Friday night and Saturday, outside major cities. Perhaps the best deal of all is a one-day conference on a Sunday. But few sponsors could persuade staff or distributors to give up a Sunday to promote business.

passing trade

In big cities, passing trade may also come into the hotel's calculation about which date would be mutually beneficial. Hotels call it 'the transient factor'. Despite the general bonhomie and good manners of most hotel salespeople, they have a shrewd idea of how to maximize their revenue. They know their busiest periods, even down to the actual day, and what level of transients they may expect to attract. If they get a group or conference enquiry, they will calculate most carefully what the profit implications are and decide on a rate accordingly.

Table 3.1 How a group booking displaces individual rooms

Day	Sun	Mon	Tue	Wed	Thur	Fri	Sat
Rooms sold	171	197	214	214	214	193	183
Forecast occupancy without group	77%	88%	96%	96%	96%	87%	82%
Group enquiry	–	–	–	30	–	–	–
Displaced individual rooms	2	10	30	30	22	8	2
					(Total over 7 days: 104)		

In the example shown in the table above, a hotel with 220 rooms receives an enquiry for 30 rooms for a conference on Wednesday. Occupancy percentage forecasts for the days within the same week range from 77 per cent on Sunday to a high of 96 per cent on Tuesday, Wednesday and Thursday, even without the conference. Because other rooms are required in the build-up to the conference and on the succeeding days, not just on the conference day, the effect of taking the Wednesday conference for 30 delegates would be to turn away 102 individual customers over the seven-day period.

When you calculate the loss of income from 104 potential individual business travellers against the lower group-rate most hoteliers levy for conference delegates, not even the additional banqueting profit would cover the profit from the 'displaced' individual bookings during this period of high occupancy.

So, in this case, the hotel may turn down the conference because they would lose the higher level of profits from the individual bookings anticipated over that period.

Most good hotels, particularly the big chains, keep meticulous records of occupancy percentages, and know exactly what revenue they might hope to achieve well in advance of the sales opportunity. So, although conferences are good business for hotels in city locations and during certain periods, individual business people will rebook many times in a year, if they like the hotel.

The issue of 'displaced' revenue may also come into play if you are trying to pitch one venue against another on the basis of cost alone. As an organizer you may feel that, by offering to hold the dinner in the hotel or by adding a cocktail party, the hotel will suddenly revise its rates. But when you realize that 80 per cent or more of a hotel's profit is based on the room rate, other elements become less important (as the diagram below shows). Banqueting, for example, is very tightly costed and only represents around 12 per cent of a hotel's profit opportunity – so reducing, say, the number of courses or choosing a 'cheaper cut' for the main course, is not going to make much difference. You would be better advised to go for added value in the shape of extra or upgraded accommodation, where the hotel will have some scope for manoeuvre.

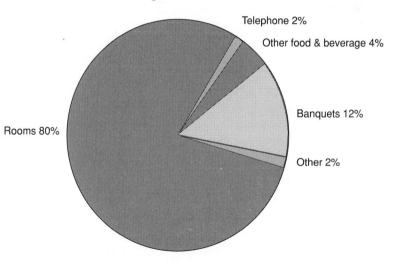

Figure 3.1 Typical chain hotel profits distribution

venue choices

There are thousands of venues to choose from, but the good news is that most of them will de-select themselves on the basis of your objectives and the profile of the potential delegates.

delegate profile

The delegate profile needs to be identified, as it has an important bearing on many aspects of conference organization – from venue choice and style of presentation to the level of catering and accommodation to be offered. Usually the delegate profile is a short statement of the level of status of the conference invitees, indicating overall numbers of delegates, as well as their age and the proportion of male to female. For example, delegates invited to a sales conference by an insurance company could be described as 200 middle-ranking managers, aged 45+, 90 per cent male. Invitees to a computer company event might be described as 50 sales people, in their 20s, 60 per cent male. It is useful for all those who have an input to the conference, at whatever level, especially the speakers, to consider the delegate profile so that arrangements made and the messages to be communicated will be suitable.

To start the whittling down process you need to take a view on a number of key questions about your event, having agreed the profile of the delegates:

- location;
- accommodation;
- programme content;
- competition.

location

Let's look at location first. Depending on where most of your delegates live, you may either be looking for a nearby venue to avoid overnight expenditure and keep travel time to a minimum, or you may deliberately wish to choose a distant venue so that the conference is perceived as a reward (but you may therefore have to provide accommodation). If efficient use of time is crucial, a city-centre location may be preferred to a country house. It is often easier to use hotels which are in big cities or near a major airport because of the public transport options rather than a remote venue which would force virtually all the delegates to use their cars or fly. As in all aspects of conference planning, you need to view the options through the eyes of the delegates. Choosing a venue in the North for a one-day conference, on the basis of getting the best financial deal, is of no use if all the potential delegates are based in the South.

roadshows

Location is particularly important when planning a series of conferences in the form of a roadshow (taking a similar message to several locations). You may find it logistically easier to choose venues near the main road network – or better still, approach the central sales reservations department of a national hotel or venue chain and negotiate an overall rate for using their properties only. When planning a roadshow, you need to bear in mind what date-span your technical crew and speaker team can cope with as they travel around. In an ideal world, for each venue, you will need one day to set-up (and rehearse if it is to be the first in a series) and one day to break down and travel to the next venue. An appreciation of the rough distances between venues should help you to decide whether you need a date-span of 7, 12 or 15 days to hold five conferences. Be aware that speakers get tired as well as the production crew. The event will be much more successful if you deliberately build in rest days, or break up the series over a weekend to give everyone a chance to rebuild their enthusiasm.

accommodation

If your conference is a one-day event, overnight accommodation may not be an issue. However, you will still probably need a small number of pre-event rooms for speakers and the technical production crew, preferably on-site. Venue selection for a one-day conference is the easiest to handle, as the choice is much wider.

However, many conferences require overnight accommodation, which tends to complicate the planning process. First you need to clarify the date-span and the number of rooms required, in addition to type of room. If the success of the conference depends on being able to offer everyone overnight accommodation (because, say, you are adding a celebratory gala dinner after the day's conference), venue choice will be restricted to a hotel which has the necessary number of bedrooms. Or you may decide that a combination of conference centre and nearby hotel would be acceptable. But you may draw the line at a conference centre and three hotels, none of which is within walking distance. There is nothing more dispiriting than a celebratory dinner brought to an abrupt halt at 11pm because the buses are leaving for the hotels.

presentation requirements

Accommodation includes having enough presentation space. You may have identified a venue with an excellent presentation room only to find that it is not available for rehearsals or set-up until midnight of the previous day. Even if you decide you can cope with this, you may discover when you turn up with your team that the previous event has over-run and you will not be able to have access until around 3 am. This may leave you with a serious problem if your conference delegates are due to arrive at 8.30am sharp, for coffee. Equally, if the nature of your presentation (a car launch, for example) means that you cannot de-rig the staging quickly, you may find yourself in breach of contract and have to pay significant charges for running over. Hotels tend to be as flexible as is possible and will judge each case on its merits, but conference centres are much less understanding if you don't keep to the letter of the contract.

space for breaks

But a conference room by itself is not enough. Normally you would expect to serve tea or coffee on arrival in a separate room or holding area before the conference begins, and often after it has finished. If the conference is all day, you will need space for lunch and any breaks. This is not usually a problem for numbers of fewer than 50, but for groups of 150 or more, the availability of a lunch room can make or break the choice of venue.

room repartition

A further factor often overlooked is the type of bedroom accommodation required – or 'room repartition', as it is termed. Your group will be used to a certain type of room when away on business, so how many single rooms and double rooms do you need? In which case, how many double rooms will you need with twin beds rather than double beds? Often the rate you negotiate will be based on access to bedrooms on a run-of-the-house basis. This means you may have to pay supplements for sea-view rooms, or executive standard rooms or suites. Few conference hotels provide a large number of single rooms these days, so you need to be prepared to use double rooms for single occupancy if the delegates cannot be asked to share.

Smoking may be another issue, and one which can seriously backfire if a vehement non-smoker has to be allocated a smoker's room situated on an all-smoking floor.

programme content

The medium is the message, as Marshall McCluhan famously said when commenting on the power of television back in the 1960s. What the venue looks like can affect how the audience perceives the message. If your main objective is to introduce cost-cutting measures and general belt-tightening, an historic home would be an unwise venue for the conference. If you are a hi-tech company with a futuristic new product to launch to the media, a tired, out-of-season resort hotel is not going to create a good impression.

On a more mundane level, if part of your programme is to involve a number of break-out sessions – which is typical of pharmaceutical conferences, for example – you need to find a venue which can offer more than just a few bedrooms with the beds taken out.

If creativity and showmanship is a vital element of the communication, venue selection may well be overridden by the technical requirements of the presentation elements. Certain products may need a minimum ceiling height or ground floor access (for trucks, for instance). If lasers or special lighting rigs are to be an integral part of the presentation, the venue must be able to support the technical equipment requirements.

The need for simultaneous translation can take up a considerable amount of room. If the venue does not already have the facility, built-in space needs to be available in the main conference room for sound-proof booths, one for each language. If one of the main format objectives is for delegates to be able to take notes, you will need enough space to seat people classroom-style, with a flat surface to write on. This will at the very least halve the space available, so you need to be sure of your numbers. To accommodate 100 delegates classroom-style you will need an approximate area of 200 square metres (2,101 square feet) but only 75 square metres (790 square feet) if you go for theatre-style seating. Many creative events call for tiered seating so that delegates can get a clearer view of the presentation. You will need to check load-bearing factors for the floor of the conference room, and ceiling height restrictions, as well as look at the health and safety regulations.

competition

If cost is a key concern, you might use facts about the competitive dynamics of the conference venue business to secure the best possible price. You might hold your conference out of season (ie not during the peak conference months), restrict delegate accommodation, arrange all the banqueting activities on-site, put up with remote locations and avoid properties with added-value (leisure clubs, golf courses, private grounds). Each of these choices will certainly drive the price down, but can also create a less convenient and enjoyable experience for delegates.

Another thought on the subject of competition is whether your delegates will be competing for service, either within the venue or in the surrounding area. Even if everything else is perfect, the presence of another large group at the venue can mean a drop in standards of service for your group. Equally a town which is bursting at the seams accommodating an international trade show, may restrict your off-site options to the extent that you have no choice but to sleep, eat, drink and breathe in the hotel, whether you like it or not.

drawing up a shortlist

Armed with your delegate profile, date-span, number of delegates, likely location, and type of presentation, you are now ready to start looking for the right venue. There is an easy way and a hard way.

By far the simplest method is to contact a venue-finding agency, which specializes in finding suitable venues for conferences and events. They draw a commission from the venue for any business placed, so as far as you, the client, are concerned, there is no cost. They will supply a list of possible options to meet your brief – and there is no doubt that this is a very effective way to get to first base.

However, by their very nature such agencies tend to be national organizations, which may not know the venue or local region in intimate detail. A way round this lack of knowledge is to contact local tourist offices, which can not only support what the venue agency has proposed but can also add local detail, such as activities near the venue, dates of competing trade fairs, other hotel options, building work which may affect access (local routes), or the facilities at the venue itself. More than one organizer has arrived on-site to find the car park being resurfaced or the main access road turned into a major traffic jam as a result of local road repairs or development. It also has to be said that some venue-finding agencies have special relationships with certain hotel chains based on volume of business placed, so you may not always get the unbiased view that you are seeking. That said, over 70 per cent of all hotel group bookings are placed by such agencies, so they must be doing something right.

other venue information sources

If you prefer to do the legwork yourself before being committed to a specific supplier or venue, there are many sources to draw on:

- ▨ venue-finding agencies;
- ▨ local tourist offices;
- ▨ hotel chains;
- ▨ trade directories;
- ▨ trade magazines;
- ▨ upmarket hotel guides;
- ▨ conference consultants;

- ■ national conference town associations;
- ■ business telephone directories;
- ■ the Internet;
- ■ conference management agencies;
- ■ production companies;
- ■ colleagues.

All major hotel chains offer a centralized venue search facility, which will take your brief and check on availability. If you know you want a Marriott or a Hilton hotel, for example, let them make the calls for you.

In most developed countries around the world, there is usually at least one comprehensive, independent guide to hotel and conference facilities. These days, not only are printed copies available in book form, but there are also CD-ROMs and, in some cases, Web sites for ease of reference. The major search engines will direct you to a suitable site, although you may have to register your details once you are connected. These references normally provide details of location, room layouts, technical data and ideal delegate numbers for group events.

The big advantage of CD-ROMs is their ability to sort venues by a number of criteria very quickly (door width, size of conference room), allowing you to home in on a likely shortlist. This would be very tedious using printed directories. Quarterly updates allow the publication of room rates so that you can sketch out a venue budget without revealing your identity. Just in case your system crashes, they also supply hard copy visual references.

Independently compiled guides can provide a useful first glance at a venue if a particular style of property is required. They are particularly good for historic homes and public buildings, which may not be listed in the more traditional directories. In addition there are a number of independent hotels which market themselves jointly (Small Luxury Hotels, for example) on a global basis to a specific audience profile.

It has to be said that the directories make money from advertising and subscription, so no directory is comprehensive. You may need to augment your research with a survey of trade magazines to uncover other properties or to get news of venues being updated or extended to take more delegates.

If all this sounds too much like hard work and you know that there will be a substantial conference staging task to be done, you may choose to give the venue search to a production company or a conference management organization. They act like a venue-finding agency in that they receive a commission from the venue so the service is free to you, the client. But because they may have actually handled projects for other clients in the venues they suggest, they often have hands-on knowledge of the venue and how it works in practice, including levels of service. The most technically correct venue is of no use if the staff do not know how to treat your delegates during the event. Like most marketing tasks, the right solution may not always be easy to access purely from desk research.

So how do you satisfy yourself that the venue will be appropriate for your needs? Simple. Go and see it.

venue inspection

Never, ever confirm a conference venue without seeing it first, even if a respected agency has convinced you that it will do the job. Only you know your own organization's culture. There may be reasons why your delegates may respond badly to the most innocuous of venues. Matching the delegate profile to your shortlist of venues requires judgement and sensitivity. In the final analysis you must decide on behalf of your organization whether the venue has the right feel for the style and tone of event you are planning. The only way to find out is to visit and do a thorough inspection.

Experienced conference organizers are able to see through the gloss, as presented by the venue sales representative, and ask the hard questions such as, 'What date are your renovation contractors due to finish the refurbishments?' Lesser mortals need, as a minimum, to check the following aspects of the venue under inspection.

inspection list

- standard bedrooms (ask to see the worst room in the house);
- proximity of kitchens to conference room (noise);
- double-glazing on conference room windows (noise);
- car parking;
- bar prices;
- availability for date-span;
- refurbishment plans;
- added value – complimentary rooms, free parking, welcome drinks;
- contract terms and conditions;
- competing clients during date-span;
- copy of a typical invoice;
- testimonials.

The inspection visit is also a two-way activity. You need to be prepared to discuss your programme, albeit in outline, and cross-check detail such as rehearsal days, access to rooms, check-out restrictions, coffee/tea break facilities, porterage policy, banqueting aspects. If you intend to take over most of the rooms in the hotel, you need to get reassurance that the kitchens can cope. A group of 250 guests all doing the same thing at the same time is very different from the behaviour of individual guests, so bottlenecks such as breakfast or room service during free time need to be looked at on a practical basis. Staffing levels, particularly in the public bar, need to be sufficient for the likely usage. It is remarkable how many hotels forget to extend their bar licence or do not put on extra waiting staff, even when they know that they may have 100 or more delegates wanting to stay up late after the gala dinner has ended, spending money.

a second opinion?

If you're in any doubt about the venue, get a second opinion. The best way to find out if a venue will work for you is to ask someone who has used it. The venue will normally be pleased to supply references from satisfied clients, so use them. But be aware that they are unlikely to supply references from dissatisfied clients. Ask colleagues if they have ever had experience of the venues under consideration. If you are a member of a trade association, contact your counterpart in another organization and ask for advice. All of the numerous trade associations will have a secretariat, which can provide the names of experienced organizers who will give you advice, often for free, on any venues you may have in mind.

So, now you have sorted out the venue, what next? Time to work on the message you expect the delegates to take home with them.

your conference checklist

- ▧ Decide a date-span. ☐
- ▧ Decide the likely location/area. ☐
- ▧ Estimate your accommodation needs. ☐
- ▧ Do a site inspection. ☐
- ▧ Get advice from professionals or colleagues. ☐

managing creativity

With the venue secure, you will need to consider what to say and how to say it.

It is a popular and believable myth that a truly creative conference can only be produced by using an expensive production house. It may indeed be that bigger ideas cost more money – but the real trick is to ensure that the appropriate idea is generated for the appropriate audience. As the conference organizer, you must manage the creative process in such a way that presentation does not relegate content to the bottom of the agenda. You are the voice of the delegate in what can be a confusing and pressurized element of the conference organization job.

go it alone – or get professional help?

You have already agreed your objectives, but should you just follow your instincts and let the content shape the presentation or should you get professional advice? More pertinently, where do you get the technical equipment to produce the show?

going it alone

For many smaller conferences, the use of an outside production house is likely to be prohibited by the costs. So, if no budget has been set aside, you will need to consider how to handle the hardware – that is, the staging, lights, microphones, projection equipment – and the software – the screen images, the speaker and what they are going to say.

Hiring equipment is relatively simple and surprisingly inexpensive. However, unless you have a background in technical production, it is somewhat daunting to decide what exactly will be required. As a layperson, you can work out that you will need two lecterns (so two fixed microphones on the lecterns), two spotlights to light them up, a screen to show the images or video, a sound system to play walk-in music and relay the speeches, a raised stage area so that delegates can see what is going on and a backdrop to act as a focal point.

It does not take long to realize that you need more than just the technical equipment. At the very least you need a technician who knows what type of equipment would be appropriate for your particular conference. Many hire companies offer this service, which, for small conferences, can be perfectly adequate – provided you can dedicate yourself on the conference day to directing the technician minute by minute as to what is going to happen next. If you need to use lights as well as sound, you will need two technicians. The job of directing both of them simultaneously usually turns out to be more than just twice as difficult. Meanwhile, the CEO wants to rehearse his opening remarks just one more time, the arriving delegates need more coffee and the video projector you have hired has just blown a fuse.

The message is simple. If you want to produce a professional presentation, you need professional help.

when to ask for help

A survey of corporate usage of production houses revealed that most corporations run five or six meetings a year, a not inconsiderable number when you realize it is dead money (fees, hire charges) with nothing to show for the cost once the conference is over (apart from the PC images used). But every event requires the appropriate level of investment.

fewer than 30 delegates

For a meeting of 30 people or fewer, the most cost-effective use of resources is to allow the hotel or venue to provide the equipment – this at least offloads on to the venue the responsibility of ensuring that it works. Often, even large hotels will hire the equipment in from a recognized local supplier who will have a vested interest in setting it up correctly. Try to make sure that you are present when the equipment is delivered so that you understand how to adjust the volume or switch it on and off. This is particularly important with video players. Check that they are compatible with the tapes you want to play and write down which channel the player has been tuned to. The most common complaint from clients to hire firms is incorrect tuning. Be aware that if you hire a large-screen video projector, it takes time to warm up and focus the image correctly – so do not leave it too late, in terms of when it is to be delivered prior to your event.

Slide projectors – the 35mm carousel variety – also need to be checked for smooth operation. The gate can become jammed, often with the hire company's logo slide, so check its operation before the technician leaves. When loading your own 35mm slides, remember to put them in upside-down and the wrong way round to ensure the correct projected image on the screen. One sophistication is to set up the projection equipment behind the screen, so that the meeting is not distracted by the sight and sound of whirring technical equipment. You will need to have ordered a screen for back projection not front projection, as these two items are designed differently.

Finally, if you have the technology to produce your images on PC, using PowerPoint or some similar system, ensure that you know how to plug in other PCs or disks, just in case speakers decide to bring their own. Not all PCs are compatible with all types of projector. Better to be safe than be unable to show the important guest speaker's slides. Always check what type of projection equipment any guest speakers will require. More than one presentation has been ruined by each speaker requiring different types of support (overheads, slides, PC) and the organizer being unable to provide all three at short notice (not to mention the inevitable disruption when the systems are switched over between speakers).

use a producer

If in doubt, or if you simply do not have the time, get in a free-lance conference producer who will take care of all the technical elements. The hotel or hardware firm will have local consultants they can suggest, depending on the type of presentation. There are a number of free advice booklets on how to use hired-in technical equipment available from the major manufacturers. The important point, if you are on your own, is to run through the programme yourself privately before the delegates get there, to check that everything works. And remember, you cannot be at both ends of the room at the same time, so think how to dim the lights if you are at the other end of the room with the projector, or outside the room organizing the coffee.

between 30 and 100 delegates

You are now entering the grey area of conference production. If it is an internal meeting, you may be able to get away with lower production values than if you were talking to distributors or outside delegates. The message may be of such burning intrinsic interest that presentation becomes secondary. It is rare. More often, the message needs to be presented properly, even internally, if it is going to have an impact. For that reason, professional help is vital with larger numbers.

Fortunately for the conference organizer, the conference production services market is a broad church. Professional support ranges from individual consultants to multinational communications agencies. Individual consultants will normally charge a time-based fee, depending on your requirement. If you simply want someone to coordinate the technical presentation on the day of the conference (which will probably include a briefing session a week or so before the event), the costs can be quite modest. However, it's more likely that consultants will be involved in the early stages, to advise on how to structure the material and plan the day's theme, to suggest outside speakers and generally to ensure that all the 'show production' elements are taken care of. As a general rule, you might appoint a conference producer two or three months before the event, having already chosen the venue. Because conference producers may well also have event management experience, they will often provide useful advice on managing venue resources 'front of house' (not the staging elements) and generally smooth your conference along. But be careful not to overload the producer. In essence, the conference producer's job is to produce a successful show or presentation. It is your job to handle the hotel and deal with the delegates – unless you appoint an outside conference organizer or event management agency.

over 100 delegates

For 100 or more delegates, you definitely need professional help, possibly even at the venue selection stage. A conference production agency is able to carry out a number of tasks which together give your message the best possible chance of being heard.

The process starts with a wide-ranging debate on your objectives, to establish a relevant creative theme. You may then consider the invitation process for delegates, in the course of which you might establish the conference logo and the overall event branding. There may be some creative options for venues other than the standard hotel options. Discussion about the content of the conference will lead to a consideration of the style of presentation and the introduction of outside speakers, special lighting, musical arrangements or technical presentation aids. You may wish to continue the event branding and theme into the gala dinner evening for continuity of the message. After the event, you may want to conduct independent research to check whether the objectives have been achieved. All these elements should be covered in any discussion with a conference production agency. This process is shown in Figure 4.1 in the flow-chart on page 49.

There are varying degrees of cost associated with the usage of expertise in any of the above areas. A minimum fee is usually around 20 per cent of total spend, and many of the larger conference production agencies will stipulate a minimum fixed fee and a variable fee based on delegate numbers before they will consider a brief. Being clear about your budget during the opening discussions will help the agency decide whether they are able to commit resources at your level of expenditure. If not, they can normally suggest a less expensive company or consultant.

the agency brief

Assuming you have already dealt with the objectives (Chapter 1), the budget (Chapter 2) and the venue (Chapter 3), you need to issue a brief to the appropriate agency. The key elements of

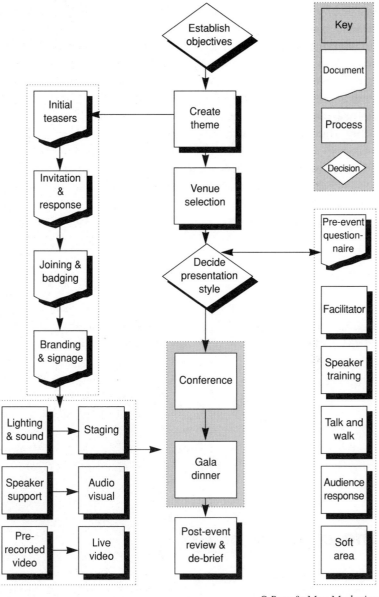

© Page & Moy Marketing

Figure 4.1 Conference production agency services

the brief will be standard and, if practicable, should be given to at least two competing agencies. The brief should cover the following areas:

- venue(s);
- date(s);
- objectives;
- delegate profile;
- number of delegates;
- likely conference content;
- past history (recent) of similar event;
- response date;
- budget guideline;
- contact for more information.

comprehensive ... but not restrictive

Your job is *not* to tell the production agency the creative answer and simply get them to work up your ideas into a visual format. The best use of the resources is for you to provide sufficient information to allow them to propose a creative response – but not so much that it cramps their creative flair.

Starting with venue, make sure that they realize what rooms you have booked (if venue selection is not part of the brief), and under what contractual restrictions. If you have agreed a contract which does not allow access to the room until midnight of the previous day, this would restrict the viability of some creative ideas. Explain whether you expect the conference theme to be carried through into the banqueting rooms or the exhibition areas, as this can eat up a considerable chunk of the budget or may offset some of the set-up costs.

Dates need to be specific and should include rehearsal and break-down periods so that the production team know how quickly they need to work. Roadshow briefs often require a leapfrogging team of two or three crews to meet the show-date parameters – and this can have a knock-on effect in terms of cost.

Objectives were fully discussed in Chapter 1, but they need to be elaborated and developed, as the creative response is usually built on the objectives. Remember to provide some background about the culture of the delegates who will attend. The creative response needs to strike a chord, not only to attract potentially reluctant attendees but also to reflect their perception of the sponsoring organization's values or intentions. Delegates from an up-market luxury goods importer are unlikely to respond to a conference theme of 'Pile it high, sell it cheap'.

Be prepared to augment your assessment of the delegate profile with more information or even anecdotal evidence. You may think that you know what service engineers in the automotive industry are like – but how might the creative response differ if one group built Rolls-Royce cars and the other produced Fords?

Delegate numbers are sometimes difficult to pin down, especially if the conference has to attract support rather than having a set number of people obliged to turn up because they are employees. Some creative solutions depend on there being manageable numbers. If you say 200 will come and 600 turn up (or could turn up) on the day, the response will need to include contingency arrangements. Annual public company meetings are a classic case in point, although they are normally undersubscribed.

Past history of a similar event for the same delegate profile, especially on video, can provide some excellent clues as to audience expectation and the level of production values you are looking for. On the other hand, it may suggest that you are not running conferences for your type of group to the standard expected by similar delegate groups in your industry, and the production company will not be shy in telling you so.

Ask for proposals to be presented in person, but do allow the agency enough time to do it justice. Three weeks should allow sufficient time, while keeping that edge of urgency. One week is simply not enough. Six weeks is probably too long, unless the response requires detailed investigation into a number of logistical issues.

Budget guidelines are essential. Not only do they provide an indication of the style and standard of event, but they also set the parameters for an appropriate creative response. If you have no idea, ring a few agencies first and ask for a ballpark figure before issuing the formal brief. Jobs at the very top end could cost millions – but these tend to be projects of national or major corporate importance, which do not come along very often, and probably include a large measure of logistics.

Finally, make sure you put in the briefing notes a contact name or names and telephone number, so that any queries can be answered. Best practice is to invite the favoured agencies to your office for a verbal briefing (independently of each other) so that they can get a feel for the culture of your business. Some organizations even feed back the answers given to individual agencies to all the competing agencies, regardless of who asked the question, to provide a completely level playing field.

What should you do if one of the agencies asks for more time? My advice would be not to stretch the date, as the way in which they respond to the pitch (on time, in a proper presentation, with a written document) is a good indication of how they would deliver your conference show. Equally, if their response is that you should not be doing a conference at all, but undertaking some other form of communication because it would be more effective, they may well be worth the wait ... but do not wait too long.

judging the proposals

You may have two or three presentations to assess. Try to get the agencies to present on the same day to the same adjudicating team. Allow one hour per presentation with half an hour between presentations, so that they can remove or set up technical equipment.

Who should attend? Preferably your main sponsor and a senior person who may be one of the speakers. To ensure fair play, you should provide a checklist to score against so that personality or good empathy does not win the day over a sound business rationale or better value for money. A typical checklist might look like this:

		Score (Marks out of 10)
1.	Presentation skills	_____
2.	Response to brief	_____
3.	Empathy	_____
4.	Costs/fee structure/value	_____
5.	Creativity	_____
6.	Documentation	_____
7.	Overall impression	_____
Agency _____	Total	_____

This list does not purport to be perfect in every case. Each conference may have a slightly different series of key factors. The important point is to do the scoring so that marks can be compared. The winner of the pitch may not turn out to be the one with the highest score, as not all the items on the list are equally important. But at the very least, such a list provides a rationale for rejecting the third-placed contender, in favour of one of the other two. From there on it will be a subjective judgement – but one not necessarily led by gut reaction to the last agency you saw.

dealing with rejection

Once your decision has been made, take time to communicate that decision professionally and promptly. Ideally, you should contact the successful agency first by telephone. Then you can write to the others with a few comments on why they were not successful. Such rejection letters are much more useful than the standard, 'On this occasion, we have decided not to proceed' – as the unsuccessful agencies have no idea where they went wrong. Any decent supplier will want to know how they could do a better job next time, so do not shrink from telling the truth. It will help them to be even hungrier next time. But avoid going into too much detail – as the last thing you want is an ongoing written or verbal debate. You have a conference to run. Two or three paragraphs stating the areas in which the agency's proposals were less good than those of the successful agency are enough (cost, creativity, feeling for the delegate profile, documentation, etc).

the conference production partnership

Depending on the budget, there are a number of areas within a presentation which need full, equal-partner discussion. Having appointed a specialist to help you with the conference presentation, take note of their advice – they have had to live with the consequences more times than you. A loose rein is better than a tight rein when it comes to getting the best value from a creative supplier.

The following four areas are likely to require joint development and agreement.

1. theme

On the surface, conference themes or event branding may seem a peripheral part of the entire conference task, but often the theme focuses everyone on the main objective and helps to provide a thread running through the entire event. There are some old favourites which seem to appear consistently, wherever or whatever the conference objectives, such as 'Simply the Best' or 'Quality Counts'.

Here are some other popular examples:

- Embark on Excellence;
- Going Places;
- Question of Quality;
- Against Adversity;
- New Horizons;
- Breaking the Barriers;
- Building on Strength;
- Today, Tomorrow – Together;
- Charting the Future;
- Committed to Quality;
- Driving Force;
- Excellence Comes as Standard;
- The Express to Success;
- Facing the Future;
- Theory into Practice;
- Go for Gold;
- Counting on Customers;
- People before Profit;
- Mission: Improvement;
- No Compromise;
- Who Dares Wins;
- Ideas in Action;
- Leading the Way;
- Future Perfect;
- Winner Takes All;
- Satisfaction Guaranteed;
- People Matter Most;
- Service First;
- The Bottom Line;
- Winning Through;
- Quest for the Best;
- On Course for Quality.

But the best examples come spontaneously and seem to suit the conference objectives exactly. Often, they alliterate (eg Route to Rewards) and have a specific relevance to the sponsoring organization (eg Better with Barclays). Within certain sectors, numbers or symbols may be enough to brand the event. Whatever your theme, you should avoid the commonplace and go for something which delivers a special message to your audience. Bespoke is always better than off-the-shelf.

2. talk with, not at

There are very few conferences which require straightforward talking at the audience with little or no feedback. Various presentational formats have therefore been devised to afford some measures of 'conversation' or feedback.

- ▨ **Chat show.** In this format, a lectern on one side of the stage may be offset on the other side by a comfortable settee with lounge chairs, taking up to six people. The idea behind this concept is to provide an alternative to the formal speech – and also to help speakers who may respond better to being interviewed than giving a formal presentation.
- ▨ **Professional linkman.** By using a professional facilitator, questions can be raised and moderated by an outsider to remove any political or sensitive bias. The linkman (or woman) can draw out the key issues without being seen to be partisan.
- ▨ **Interactive response.** There are a number of audience reaction devices, made popular by television gameshows, which can help gauge reaction and focus discussions. Delegates make choices anonymously, in their seats, to agree or disagree with a proposition from the presentation area so that the real issues can be brought out into the open, usually in graphic format on a big screen.
- ▨ **Panel sessions.** Although somewhat hackneyed and over-used in some industries, an old-fashioned panel session does at least provide a bridge between the technical experts and the delegates. Due to natural audience reticence, questions often have to be planted to get the debate going. However, because the questioners by definition identify themselves, the level of debate tends to be fairly bland and uncontroversial.

▨ **In the round.** This format involves the delegates being seated much closer to the speaker, perhaps on three sides. The presenter answers questions directly from the audience (or sometimes channelled through a moderator). This format requires strong communicators who are quick on their feet and able, politely, to deflect any potentially aggressive lines of questioning. This is a high-risk option with an inexperienced presenter and some coaching of speakers may be required.

3. pre-shot modules

During the development phase, a number of issues may need to be researched or information collected before the presentation. One way of allowing honest discussion is to prepackage the issue in the form of a news-style report, often including comments on video from ordinary delegates as the starting point. 'Vox pops', as they are known, help to build empathy with the conference audience and to put forward the view of the 'man in the street', so that the issues of ordinary delegates can be seen to have been explored.

Another type of pre-shot module can be useful for the launch of a new product or service: here, multimedia are used in a prepackaged sequence to present the benefits creatively.

One advantage of creating these mini-presentations beforehand is that you can ensure identical high standards (especially important in a roadshow) and provide quality of communication, however well or badly the supporting live speakers perform. A further advantage, especially in these days of multinational communication, is the opportunity to offset marketing costs by creating a generic video which can be overdubbed into other languages for international presentation. This also provides continuity of style and content, which can otherwise be lacking when a company is attempting to roll out an important message across an international network.

4. *coup de théâtre*

At the top end of the budget scale, the whole staging of the event (in a circus ring, ship, space – even inside a bottle!) could be the theme which conveys a powerful message. Or revealing the new product could be a spectacular theatrical display involving scissor-lifts, sudden reveals, expensive lighting rigs or well-known personalities. This type of *coup de théâtre* ('theatrical strike', literally) can be very effective if it relates to the main objective, but a bit of a distraction if it is merely a way of drawing attention to a minor issue of the agenda.

A *coup de théâtre* does not always need to cost large amounts of money – although they often do. A computer company, which specialized in back-up security systems, dramatized their product by using a tight-rope walker to walk over the audience, first without a safety net, then with a safety net. The cost was minimal, but delegates were forced to assimilate the main message: the safety net removes the risk of disaster, even though you have every confidence that the tightrope walker will not fall.

managing the speakers

External speakers, if you are paying them a fee, are relatively straightforward. No doubt they have been chosen for the relevance of their message or their entertainment value. It is vital that you, as the conference organizer, know in broad terms what they are going to say and how they are going to say it. They need to support the main theme or main objective and, if required, to have adequate supporting material to blend into your day's programme. You will be surprised at how few celebrity speakers, particularly of the motivational kind, have inadequate support material, so ensure that you see beforehand what they intend to use, to avoid embarrassment. Costs can vary a great deal for, say, 45 minutes of presentation – so check your budget before getting too enthusiastic.

Internal speakers may prove to be more problematical. Few internal speakers are professional presenters, used to addressing large audiences on a regular basis. Technical experts often prove to be the worst at putting over their message, despite having a message that the audience generally wants to hear. Each internal speaker needs specific handling to get the best out of them. You may need to use a variety of techniques to aid the communication task, from speaker training to television prompt systems.

Be prepared to chase internal speakers doggedly for their scripts. Be particularly suspicious of any speaker who declares that they will write what they have to say on the weekend before the event, and will not need images or supporting material. Your job is to make them look good on the day, often in spite of themselves. As a general rule, scripts should be available at least four weeks before the event so that the production company can tailor suitable support material. You should certainly schedule a rehearsal, either off-site a few days before or on-site on the day before, to ensure that everyone is aware of what others are saying. There is often a need to fine-tune the scripts for emphasis when several speakers realize, perhaps for the first time, that they have covered the same issue or presented conflicting views.

creating a balance

The final element of show production is to look at the balance of the day to see, from a delegate viewpoint, how the day is panning out. You may have several different elements which need to come across as a logical, thought-through progression of ideas, leading to a positive conclusion. Conference producers can help you to decide the best mix, from their previous production experience, but only you can decide.

Perhaps the most important element is how to pace the day so that you end on a natural high.

Here is a good working model for a day conference:

Opening sequence

 1. Establish theme;
 2. Introduce medium-level topic;
 3. Present high-interest topic;

Break

 4. Invite discussion;
 5. Announce minor news;

Luncheon

 6. Audience feedback, vox pops;
 7. Technical briefing;
 8. Present highest-level interest topic;
 9. Launch exciting news.

Close

In this way you will create specific peaks of interest and build up to the high points in a managed way.

conclusion

Conference production is both a science and an art and although as conference organizer you are not expected to create or produce every single element yourself, you need to manage the process so that both sponsors and delegates get the most relevant message at reasonable cost.

your conference checklist

 ▓ Brief several conference production agencies. ☐
 ▓ Appoint a conference production agency. ☐
 ▓ Decide the creative theme. ☐
 ▓ Create a balanced show. ☐

event management and logistics

Now that your brief to the conference production agency has set the creative side in motion, you can concentrate on the core task – event management.

But what does event management include? Although there are few books on it and even fewer articles about it, event management is the cornerstone of every conference. It covers everything which makes the delegate feel more receptive to the conference messages, except the communication of the message itself. Typically it may cover the following areas:

- invitation process;
- travel arrangements;
- delegate reception;
- breaks;
- luncheon;
- list management.

Event management deals with the logistics and hygiene factors which create the right environment for a positive reception of the conference message. At the lowest level, it would be counterproductive, for example, to run a conference with a theme,

'Good Profits come from Good Planning', if it were logistically impossible to get all the delegates to the venue in time for the CEO's opening conference remarks. At a higher level, a relaxed audience is a receptive audience and is more likely to support the policy statements of the conference sponsors. When delegates have niggling complaints about comfort factors, such as seating, food or their hotel room, no amount of sophisticated presentation from the main stage will make them forget it. Many an excellent conference production has been ruined by poor attention to event management issues.

It all starts with the invitation process.

the invitation process

If the conference is to be a smooth integration of input from various people, you should start as you mean to go on, with an efficient and professional invitation process. This is all about raising the right level of expectation. Either by yourself or with the production company, you will have decided on the name or theme for the conference. This branding may well appear for the first time on the invitation communication. This must be well presented so that delegates will want to attend. More importantly, it must encourage those who need to be influenced to attend, such as distributors and third parties.

The invitation is not only a way of saying, 'Come to our show'. It is also a device to confirm the name and contact address of the delegate, perhaps gather other relevant information at the same time, and open up a potential dialogue for further communication, before, during and after the conference. So where do you start? With a database.

database development

To communicate with the potential invitees, you need to build a suitable database from any raw lists which may be available. If you are inviting employees, the usual cascade channels may be sufficient (managers telling managers who tell staff). However, you still need to ensure that everyone knows when the conference takes place (even those who happen to be on holiday at the time of the invitation). It helps to know who is coming and the level of general support so you can estimate correct numbers for parking, banqueting and overnight rooms.

The best advice is to adapt the employee list from payroll, mail a hard-copy invitation, personalized to each invitee, and record acceptances. In that way you know who is not coming, so that you can chase attendance through the management line. If you are on e-mail or a similar personnel communication system, this can be done electronically – but you still need to chase up the non-respondents to help you to plan efficiently.

There are many software products available to gather delegate data and produce statistical analyses of potential attendance. Investment in this area is crucial if you manage more than, say, three events a year. The packages often include useful features, such as seating plans or delegate badges, to help with the administration of the invitees through the system.

third-party invitees

For third parties and distributors who are not your employees, the task is somewhat harder. They have their own businesses to run and may well consider time spent at your event as potentially wasted. A database may not exist or may be badly maintained. In this event, you need to include a list-building or list-cleaning exercise into your plan, through a professional tele-contact team, or be prepared to second a few secretaries to spend several days getting the right names, titles, telephone numbers and addresses. There is nothing worse than an incorrectly addressed invitation, especially if potential delegates feel that they could be doing something more constructive with their time. It is vital to gather many more potential names than you require. Unless delegates desperately need to acquire the information you are going to impart at the conference, acceptances can be as low as 25 per cent – and the last thing you need is a conference room which is only a quarter full, because of the effect of the gaps in the audience on those who have taken the trouble to attend. Clearly the level of hospitality and the quality or location of the venue will have a powerful effect on attendance numbers. Spouse or partner invitations improve acceptances dramatically, but there are clearly additional cost implications.

the invitation mailing

What information should you divulge at the invitation stage? You need to give enough to encourage acceptance but not so much that delegates decide they can get the same information in some other way than attending the conference. Creativity in terms of presentation and graphics can arouse curiosity and interest in such a way that non-attendance is simply not an option.

But there are some basic logistical details you need to provide so that potential delegates can make up their minds.

elements to include on the invitation

- ▓ name, title, address of delegate;
- ▓ date, location of conference; map, rail/road/air connections;
- ▓ start time (so they can plan their outward journey);
- ▓ finish time (so they can plan their return journey);
- ▓ theme (reason for conference);
- ▓ guest speakers (if attractive or famous);
- ▓ personalization from conference sponsor;
- ▓ simple reply device;

space for delegates to supply useful personal information (telephone number, e-mail address, dietary needs, special disability needs, specific interests).

One relatively recent innovation is the creation of a plastic card, like a credit card, with the delegate's name already inscribed on the face as part of the invitation. When removed from its housing, the card can be used in conjunction with a swipe machine on entry to the event as a badge, to avoid manual registration and queuing, as well as to keep count electronically of who has registered. This device can also act as a strong prompt to confirm attendance, especially if a reply telephone or e-mail address is given on the back of the card itself.

timing is important

Reminders should be built into your invitation plan, as telephone callbacks, e-mail or further direct mail. Each event will have its own optimum time for invitation acceptance. Some people need to be approached three months before the event. In other circumstances, three to four weeks may be the optimum time. As conference organizer, you need to think through the process from the delegate's viewpoint so that you can implement your invitation and reminders plan at the most effective time. Invitations sent out too close to the event, or during August, are unlikely to achieve the response levels you need to confirm relevant details to the venue. For a third-party, non-employee event, you should certainly plan to arrange reminders in the final two weeks to encourage the undecided to attend.

confirming attendance

Your most precious invitees are those who have accepted. You need to build a communication channel with them leading up to the event, to reduce the inevitable drop-out rate. Even if the conference involves them in no personal or corporate cost, confirmed delegates must be maintained and this takes consideration and planning.

Confirmed acceptances need to be filed separately from other potential attendees, and you must communicate with them on a regular basis. Your communications can include e-mail messages, telephone contact, more detail about the programme content when it becomes available, joining instructions (travel details, timings, badging and registration) and hospitality invitations for use during the conference event.

Once you have built up a rapport with the confirmed attendees, you can use them to suggest other people in a similar category who might benefit from your conference invitation. 'Delegate-get-delegate' schemes can be the most cost-effective way to improve attendance, especially if time is running out and you need to boost attendance quickly.

travel arrangements

For most conferences travel is up to the delegate – but if travel is a key factor for good attendance, you need to consider what you can do to make it less of a barrier.

Within the world of association and trade conferences, numerous techniques have been tried over the years to encourage attendance. Free exhibitor guides, technical books, calculators, software disks, discounts on hotels, rooms, restaurant vouchers, watches, wine and many other types of incentive have been offered. One of the most effective devices has been to provide free travel or overnight accommodation under the guise of the event's own travel club. But everything has its price, and unless you can get a sponsor to underwrite the discount or the cost, it can be expensive. A further hidden cost is the organizational time it takes to negotiate the discount, find a sponsor and confirm the details of the arrangements to participating delegates. Individual itineraries for 100 or more

VIPs can be very time-consuming as any business travel agent will tell you, so before you commit yourself to this technique to build attendance, consider carefully how badly you need these specific attendees.

employee travel

For closed groups of employees, the aim of organizing the travel is less to attract attendance than to ensure that the conference starts on time and to keep expenses under control. Imagine a national conference for 500 members of the sales-force. If everyone charged business mileage on their own cars, the cost could significantly overrun the conference budget. In addition, most large companies treat individual expenses as separate from marketing costs, so often the cost of internal travel to such an event remains hidden until the year end when it is too late to do anything about it. The sensible approach is to take on the travel logistics as part of the conference organization task, and include it in the budget.

trains, buses and planes

In your deliberations about venue selection, you will have kept one eye on the distribution of your likely delegates. Now that the venue has been chosen, you need to consider the most cost-efficient way to get the delegates there and back. The railway network could be your first option, as good discounts are available for group travel, either to a single location from a variety of starting points or on a charter.

Bus companies with a national network offer a similar service whereby delegates can be picked up at pre-arranged places. With private charters you are able to upgrade the catering services or show specific videos *en route* to create the desired atmosphere before and after the event. Insist on radio or mobile phone contact with the driver so that, in the event of an accident or bad weather, you can be informed of any delays and decide whether to start the conference without the delayed delegates.

For smaller groups, there may be chauffeur companies which can provide a range of smaller vehicles. Depending on the cost and distances involved, two smaller vehicles may be less expensive than one large one, if the large one turns out to be less than half full. Standard seat availability goes from 8 to 12, 18, 36 and 49. Unlike trains, buses can travel door to door, but you need to ensure that everyone knows how to locate their transport for the return journey to avoid the majority of prompt travellers being delayed by the minority who fail to show at the stated departure time.

far-flung delegates

However central the venue, there will inevitably be small groups of delegates who cannot get to the conference venue for a one-day conference unless they travel by air or come the day before. Often, it is because they live in an area not well served by scheduled transport rather than the actual distance involved. You may consider overnight accommodation before the conference to be a more cost-effective option than a same-day return air fare, depending on the day of the week.

Start and finish times for the conference itself may well be dictated by the travel schedules of certain types of delegates, especially if it is a one-day conference – so take care not to be too prescriptive too early on in your planning. A 10 am start with a 4.30 pm finish may be necessary to accommodate a national delegate profile: people not only need time to get there but may need to leave early for return connections. It is poor planning and very disruptive to have a block of delegates leaving the conference mid-afternoon to catch a travel connection, just when the day's programme is reaching its climax. If this is inevitable, seat them near the back exit doors to minimize the disruption. Group discounts for travel may be available for 10 or more individuals, so if you can get delegates to convene at one central location and use one company rather than two or more, this can help to minimize the overall cost.

delegate reception

First impressions count, especially if your delegate has difficulties getting to the conference. There are a number of logistical elements you need to consider to ensure a seamless transition from arrival to conference room. In the case of delegates arriving independently, car parking is crucial. In an ideal world, the delegate should be able to park within easy walking distance of the main entrance. In the case of large hotels and conference centres, this is rarely the case. As the conference organizer you need to have walked through the process yourself to see how you can make it easier.

When you do the venue site inspection, ask about the car parking system and explore ways to improve upon simply turning up and hoping for the best. Some venues will designate and rope off certain areas for your delegates, if space allows. If there is a nearby conference-centre car park you can negotiate a concessionary day-rate, but delegates will need to show an agreed business card or conference invitation to qualify. You may consider a private bus shuttle from car park to conference venue, especially if it is likely to be bad weather. Take care not to be fooled on your site inspection as to how quiet the car park is, as you may be visiting on a non-conference day. If you cannot secure private parking, find out where delegates can park safely and enclose a diagram in the invitation mailing, if necessary. Go by car yourself to the venue, and try out the system to find the best procedure – then multiply it by the number of delegates. If the conference centre's security system takes two minutes per car on entry, it will take 100 delegates over three hours to gain access. There is bound to be an alternative procedure, so ask about it. Some venues restrict bus access to the main entrance, so ask about this and agree a sensible compromise, remembering to inform the drivers of the agreed system.

meet and greet

Once inside the venue delegates look for two things: something they recognize and cloakrooms. Clear signage can do much to alleviate the anxieties of latecomers who may get disproportionately irritated if they cannot easily find the conference room, especially in a large hotel or conference complex. The name or theme of the conference and the sponsor is enough to get instant recognition. Subject to the inevitable venue restrictions, make your signage big and bold. Remember to check with reception, if it is a hotel, that they have your organization's name correct. It is not unusual to find the name of the venue-finding agency or the conference production house on the day plan, simply because they may have originally booked the venue. In the case of a conference centre, you have much more freedom to brand the entrance with flags, banners and posters.

Notwithstanding the need for adequate security (you do not want just anybody attending your conference), you need to provide an immediate presence for the delegate. This means a reception or registration facility separate from the standard venue reception. If delegates have been issued with badges in advance, you will need to provide the facility to create new badges on site quickly. On average, 10 per cent of delegates will fail to bring their badge or documentation, so be prepared.

registration staffing levels

If delegates need to register on site, you will need one member of staff per 50 expected delegates. This will keep queuing down to a minimum, especially if each delegate needs to complete a registration form. Allow for a few extra staff to be free to float, so that queries can be answered without delegates having to queue first. Ideally cloakroom facilities need to be available before registration to keep unnecessary queuing to a minimum.

There is no right or wrong way to facilitate the registration process. It depends on the delegate profile and the expected time-span during which they are likely to register. For your own staff events, you may not wish to have a formal registration process, other than providing badges and distributing an agenda. A good system is to split the arrivals into alphabetical groups (A–E, F–L, etc), clearly signposted so that delegates can pre-sort themselves before arriving at the desk. Lay the badges out alphabetically facing the registration staff, as reading badges upside-down is an acquired skill, especially in our increasingly multiracial society. It also stops badges being taken by impatient delegates who then may not receive some essential item of printed information or an important message. If a badge is missing or incorrect, have a separate facility to deal with it rather than holding up the entire queue. Be aware that if you have organized group travel, the delegates will, by definition, arrive in blocks, so be prepared to cope. As for timings, you should be ready to 'badge' at least one hour before the conference – in any large group of delegates a significant minority always turns up early.

One other advantage of a badging system is that, once the conference has begun, it provides an instant count of who has not yet arrived and who did not turn up. Keep a record of these 'no-shows' as you may need to find out why after the event.

giving out materials

Depending on the level of interaction required, you should try to keep the distribution of materials at registration to a minimum, preferably doing the distribution in advance or as delegates enter the conference room. Under no circumstances should you provide verbatim scripts or copies of images before the presentations have been made. Not only does this create unnecessary logistical problems, but it also provides an excuse for some delegates (dare we say, the media in particular?) not to attend the conference at all in the hope that they can read the scripts later. They may miss the vital points or mood of the conference if they merely read the planned scripts. It also inhibits the presenters, who sometimes need to abandon their prepared scripts if issues brought up in earlier sessions need to be addressed live. Training conferences are different. The scripts and images may act as an aid to understanding if there is little or no interaction possible. If in doubt, always distribute literature at the end of the conference as delegates leave.

create a holding area

A key element of any conference is the opportunity for delegates to meet with peers or industry colleagues. Try not to make it difficult. Within your programme you need to build in times when delegates can simply relax and chat. After registration is one such opportunity. Delegates should have the chance to get refreshments (especially if they have had a long journey), use the cloakroom facilities and socialize. This period also provides the conference organizer with a degree of flexibility regarding the start time of the conference, in case of transport delays or show production problems. Final technical show rehearsals may be going on, and the conference producer may need that extra five minutes to clarify lighting cues or do sound checks. Starting a few minutes late is better than starting on time but ill-prepared, not knowing whether or not that important opening sequence is going to work.

entering the conference room

If you are catering for a large number of delegates, you may wish to direct them to particular entry points according to a number or colour code on their badges. Alternatively they could be separated into upper, middle and lower holding areas so that entry time to the conference room is reduced.

For smaller conferences, entry can be *ad hoc* – but bear in mind that even 200 people normally take around 10 minutes to enter and be seated, so build this into your schedule. You should post sponsor representatives or security personnel at the entry points to discourage delegates from gaining early access. Last-minute rehearsals may be going on, particularly set-piece sections such as the launch of a new product, and you could do without even a small number of delegates being privy to the details in advance.

As delegates enter the conference room, the aim should be to establish the conference theme and mood immediately. Ambient music, relevant light settings and a generally calm atmosphere are preferred. Avoid placing agenda notes or litera-ture on the seats – these will be dropped on the floor quite rapidly and will only serve as a distraction from activity on the main stage. If speakers or VIPs are to be seated in the auditorium, reserve a row, or part of a row, at the front for them, and have a team member standing by to enforce the seating plan. If award winners are to be called up on stage, seat them in the correct sequence near the front so that they have clear and easy access to the stage at the relevant time.

It is inevitable that delegates will stand around their seats and chat. You need to agree a simple signal for the start of the conference with the conference producer. You must be in contact with the entry-point staff to know when all the dele-gates have moved into the conference room, and with the conference producer who may be backstage or up in the projec-tion area at the back of the auditorium. A simple thumbs up may suffice, but it is more professional to be linked up on head-phones or a mobile phone, so that you can speak directly without drawing attention to yourself.

It is rare for a conference to start exactly on time, or for everyone who said they would come to attend. By knowing beforehand who is due to attend, and by quickly glancing at the remaining delegate badges, you can take a view as to whether to start without the no-shows or wait. If a significant number has not arrived, it is usually because they are travelling together as a group and your logistical planning (buses with radio or mobile contact) will have ensured that you know how long they are likely to be delayed.

dealing with latecomers

Once the conference room doors have been closed, it is your job, as the conference organizer, to deal with late arrivals. A common format for the beginning of a conference is to have a short opening sequence or scene-setting speech. Make sure that the registration staff have a copy of the agenda so that they can tell late delegates what point the conference is likely to have reached. Entry-point staff should be given clear instructions as to when to allow latecomers in, or whether they should be redirected to a particular entry point at the back of the auditorium. Latecomers wandering in near the front of the stage are distracting both for speakers and audience.

handling the breaks

Conferences are dynamic occasions. They do not always run to schedule because, in the heat of the moment, speakers take more or less time than they did in rehearsal, and interactive sessions with the audience often take longer than anticipated. It is crucial to keep a running check on how things are progressing in the conference room so that preparations for the first break in the programme can be timely. As conference organizer, you may decide to skip in and out of the conference room and make contact backstage with the day facilitator to see if the programme is running longer or shorter than planned (this section is based on a one-day conference). One of the advantages of being involved in the conference production element is that you will know what is coming up in the programme, enabling you to form your own judgement. Some organizers rely on the conference producer to provide a 10-minute warning before a break, but this is not always practicable and, in the heat of the live event, may well be something that gets forgotten.

Why do you need to know? It sounds obvious, but not all venues are able to keep refreshments hot indefinitely or create refreshments in large quantities instantly. If this is the case with your venue (which you will have checked during the site inspection), you may need to bring forward the scheduled break time and warn the catering or banqueting staff accordingly. In your build-up to the conference, it is wise to tell the day facilitator that you will be working to a specific schedule for breaks, and that if the schedule needs to be changed, you will need at least 30 minutes notice. It creates a bad impression if delegates break from the conference to find no refreshments and, even worse, hospitality staff looking confused and badly prepared.

The first break creates the same people-moving problems as the conference opening. The length of the break needs to be at least 30 minutes, as exit and re-entry could take as long as 15 minutes for a large group. For smaller groups you can afford to be more parsimonious. Catering staff should be briefed on the time available so that they can pace their speed of service. Adding more service points and staff for the relevant 15 minutes can make all the difference between an efficient break and an irritating interruption in the eyes of the delegates.

luncheon

Once the delegates are back in the conference room, you need to check on the arrangements for luncheon. From your pre-registration exercise, you will know your maximum numbers and your special diets. If the no-shows have been minimal, leave the plans as they are. From a catering point of view, it makes little difference with a few hours to go. However, if the numbers are significantly down (or up in some circumstances), the quicker you review the plan the better. It is clearly easier to cater down than cater up at short notice, but forewarned is forearmed.

Once again, do not underestimate how long it takes to get people seated and serve a meal: 45 minutes is too short for a sit-down meal, even if you throw serving staff at the problem. An hour and a half could be deemed to be too long, unless one of your objectives is to provide plenty of time for social inter-action. As conference organizer you need to keep a wary eye on the time. If, for whatever reason, the meal finishes early you will need to have created a holding area for the delegates until the conference production team is ready. Delegates should not be allowed in the conference room during luncheon, as this is usually the only time the conference production team has to fine-tune the set pieces for the afternoon session.

event information

The role of the event management support team, after the registration task and during the day, is to provide information and act as host. There is no real need to retain all the staff used at registration, but those who remain need to be able to provide accurate and timely information about the programme and the venue. Typical questions will revolve around the following topics:

- ▓ delegate list (attendees/no-shows);
- ▓ sponsor brochures, other material;
- ▓ conference agenda, timings;
- ▓ venue map, facilities, telephones;
- ▓ travel connections, local information.

If you have a choice, use your own staff rather than an agency staff after registration – the emphasis will then be on knowledge of the sponsor and hosting rather than pure administrative efficiency.

departure management

Having kept in contact with what is going on in the conference room during the afternoon, you should be preparing your team to organize a smooth departure from the venue.

If you have been responsible for return transport, you need to have transfers standing by, up to 30 minutes before the expected finish time, so that delegates can walk directly from the conference to their return transport. If they are returning by bus, this will involve keeping in contact with the bus company and ensuring that all the relevant buses are standing by. If access is restricted either by space or by local regulations, you need to keep delegates in a holding area with refreshments until their bus is available and called. It is often a good idea to serve refreshments after the event as this tends to stagger departures, which reduces queuing at all the bottleneck points (cloakrooms, taxis, stairways). In some venues you need to be aware that other groups may be using the facilities on the same evening, so indefinite hospitality is not possible. People must be moved along politely but firmly to avoid possible penalty payments to the venue.

delegate list management

Before you leave the venue, keep as much information about the delegates as you can, either manually or on disk, to help you plan an even better event next time.

You will have an alphabetical list of invitees, a list of no-shows, a possible list of attendees on the day who were not on

the original list of invitees, as well as other details such as
seminar topic choices, special diets, requests for more information and requests for meetings with specific employees of the
sponsor.

By careful correlation of delegate details, you can build
personal profiles of each delegate which, over time, could be a
valuable marketing tool for the future if they are third-party
distributors or important buyers.

Even for employee delegates, it may be useful for managers
to know who did not attend so that they can take any necessary
action. More generally, the data can provide a starting point
for post-event research (see Chapter 9) and for an improvement
plan for the following year's conference.

budget verification

Your final port of call should be to the venue manager's office
to check on any extras or catering amendments. If there is any
dispute, it is better to query anomalies on the day while the
detail is fresh in everyone's mind. Trying to prove three weeks
later that additional charges were not sanctioned is a tall order.
It is particularly important to tackle this job on the day when
you are dealing with conference centres, as they always have
many more ways of charging extra than hotels.

clean up ... and go

Before you finally go off with your support team to celebrate a
job well done, remove any sensitive material left lying around
in the hospitality areas or under the registration tables. If it is
highly confidential information, you may even want to
check out the cloakrooms. If you come across personal items
left behind by delegates, take them to security but do not
forget to leave your business card with security and the cloakroom attendant, as delegates often contact the venue first and

you second, as soon as they realize they have left something behind.

your conference checklist

▒ Devise the invitation. ☐
▒ Organize the travel logistics. ☐
▒ Decide how to register delegates. ☐
▒ Plan the breaks procedure. ☐
▒ Do a final sweep of the venue. ☐

accommodating your conference

When you choose a hotel, you will already have a broad view of your accommodation requirements. There are three main areas to consider when a hotel accommodates a conference: the conference room, banqueting and the capacity to offer delegates appropriate overnight facilities. Now you need to get down to the detail to see if the event you are running can be made to fit into the available space.

conference capacity

Unlike overnight accommodation, the space you book for the conference is fixed. The golden rule at the outset is to opt for a larger area than you need on the basis that you can always arrange the stage area and the seating in such a way as to minimize extra space. What you cannot do is squeeze in more delegates than will comfortably fit. You can solve the problem with a one-day conference by running two half-day conferences back to back, bisected by lunch – but this is at best an emergency solution to an oversubscribed conference.

There are some standard tables and charts you can use to estimate how much space you will need. Most good conference venues will have done the work for you – they publish room capacities for both front and back image projection and for different types of seating arrangement. But just in case they do not publish such information or you want to double-check that they have got it right, here are some guidelines.

production needs

When planning the conference room layout, you need to start by looking at which space to reserve for image projection, and the location of essential power. You might also consider whether the spill of daylight from windows would determine where to place the screen, however well draped the room is. A further consideration is access to the room by delegates: if possible, the screen should be set up at the opposite end to their entrance, or to the side of it, to minimize disruption from possible latecomers.

If you are using front projection, as a general rule, delegates should be no closer than twice the screen height in order to be able to see the images clearly. The bottom of the screen should be no lower than 1.2 metres (4 feet) from the ground, so that everyone seated can see the screen above other people's heads. You may need to allow for the screen to be tilted forward at the top to correct 'keystoning' (a tapering of the image on the screen due to the angle of image projection). You should also be aware that there are optimum viewing angles, which can change depending on how close you are to the screen. The end seats on the front row, for example, may be at too acute an angle to facilitate good viewing, and you may have to 'lose' a row or two to ensure that everyone can see clearly.

For rear or back projection, the same rules apply, but you need to add the space required behind the screen for throwing a clear image. Often up to one-third of the length of the conference room will be required to project a rear image, although you can 'fold' the image by using mirrors to take up less space.

Room heights can cause a real problem for image projection, because a low ceiling restricts the height of the top of the image. Heads will start to get in the way of the image projection if the ceiling is too low. About 3 metres (9 feet) is an acceptable minimum ceiling height for front projection for a moderately sized meeting. Any lower and you will have to use back projection. When doing the calculations, you need to bear in mind the effect of any hanging chandeliers or ceiling decorations when it comes to the feasibility of projecting an unencumbered image.

There is a range of projection equipment available to make the best use of the available 'throw' and to give clear image definition. It is important to brief the production company or the in-house technician carefully on the type of images to be shown (speaker support, video, satellite feed, live computer data, etc), so that they can advise on the best possible system at lowest cost.

In terms of essential power, most banqueting information packs which include room layouts will show the position of the main power points and often the ambient lighting switches, so that you can choose a relevant projection site. Ideally you would not wish to run cabling through an audience area, but you would want to be able to control ambient lighting on an *ad hoc* basis from the entry/exit point, so you could adjust the lighting at the beginning and end of sessions.

One final point about technical equipment is easy access. If you have a choice, opt for the ground floor every time. Lifts get stuck or are simply not switched on late at night to save power, and the dimensions of the lift, even a service lift, are often inadequate to take items of staging and scenery. Make things easy for the technical crew to set up and de-rig, and half the battle is won.

conference room layouts

There are a dozen or so different ways to arrange conference seating, either to fit more people in or to create a specific ambience for delegate and speaker communication (as shown in the diagram opposite). Not all venues use the same terms so it is as well to know what you mean so that the venue can acknowledge whether it has understood.

The most common forms are:

- **Schoolroom, ordinary.** Delegates face the screen behind rows of desks, usually with a central aisle for ease of access. Leave about a metre (3 feet) between tables to allow for seating.
- **Schoolroom, perpendicular.** Same idea, but have the stage to the side.
- **Schoolroom, V-shaped.** Same as ordinary schoolroom but arranged in a herringbone pattern, so delegates get a slightly better view of each other.
- **Theatre/auditorium.** Front-facing, in rows, no desks in between.
- **Theatre, V-shaped.** As above, but arranged in a herringbone pattern.
- **Board of directors.** Seating around a long table with one or two at either end.
- **Hollow square.** Seating with delegates facing each other on all four sides of a square.
- **U-shape.** Sometimes known as wedding banquet; delegates occupy five sides of a six-sided U-shape.
- **Cabaret.** Delegates sit at round tables, as if for a dinner, but may only occupy half of each table.

Different layouts can make a significant difference to the numbers you can accommodate. It is clear from the diagram on p.84 that you can get over twice as many conference delegates in the room by switching from classroom to theatre style, so before you opt automatically for tables, ask yourself if you really need them.

Hollow Square

U-shape

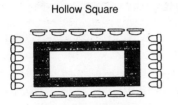

Boardroom

Theatre

Classroom

Banquet with spur

Oval

Round 10s

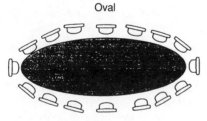

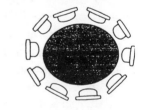

Cabaret-style

Herringbone

Figure 6.1 Room layouts

In all these layouts, hotels have usually allowed for access space around the perimeters, although if you intend to arrange buffet tables around the walls for later, take care not to block any fire and safety exits.

It is necessary to offer a word of caution about the increasing number of historic houses and private residences coming on to the conference market. It is wise to be sceptical about measurements and scale floor-plans, if space is critical. Features such as bay windows, pillars, balconies and staircases will reduce available conference space and sight-lines for delegates. You may also find that power sources are rarely in the most convenient places, so a thorough site inspection with a tape measure is recommended. And watch out for chandeliers which cannot be removed.

make room

No one knows exactly how many delegates will attend a large conference, nor can you always, at the beginning of a project, be completely accurate about the staging arrangements. Flexibility is crucial if you have to accommodate more delegates than planned, but do not simply crowd them into the front or back of the auditorium. Talk to your production house to see if any staging changes could create more space. Often it can be done quite easily, provided the production house realizes it is a problem. If in doubt, pay for a technical layout drawing to be absolutely sure, using the hotel's technical floor-plans, not the brochure designs reprinted, often erroneously, in banqueting packs. It is easier to make more room in your conference room through pre-planning than by hoping for the best on the day.

overnight accommodation

When you did your venue inspection, you will have taken note of the room repartition (number and type of different rooms) for overnight accommodation. Although hotels have all kinds of internal names for the types of room on offer, these tend to fall into standard, industry-wide categories.

- ▦ **Single room.** A room for single occupancy with one bed, normally a double bed, but could be narrower.
- ▦ **Double room.** A room for two occupants sleeping in the same bed.
- ▦ **Twin room.** A room for two occupants, sleeping in separate beds.
- ▦ *En Suite.* Toilet and shower-room or bathroom are an integral part of the room.
- ▦ **Executive.** Large double or twin, sometimes with a work desk or sitting area, upgraded amenities such as trouser-press, or higher quality toiletries, for example.
- ▦ **Suite.** A room with a separate living area.
- ▦ **Presidential suite.** The best suite in the hotel, usually with two or three bedrooms and a number of living rooms, often with a private kitchen/wet bar.

There are some room types whose names have been borrowed from other parts of the world, such as:

- ▦ **Cabana.** A room near or next to the pool, with or without sleeping accommodation.
- ▦ **Lanai.** A room with a balcony or patio, overlooking water or a garden (of Hawaiian origin).
- ▦ **Studio.** A room with one or two settees which convert into beds.

Some hotel properties charge a premium for corner-sited rooms, because they tend to offer better views or more space. Rooms on the top floor are often of better quality than on other floors, and many hotels these days have created 'executive floors' with dedicated breakfast and business facilities. No-smoking floors are becoming increasingly popular, as are women-only floors.

But take time to understand the terminology, as each hotel is different. One man's suite can be another man's cabana, unless you are persistent and check exactly what each one includes.

On your site inspection, make a comprehensive list of what type of rooms there are and how many are undergoing refurbishment. Be very specific about suites, as normally such rooms are scarce and you need to book them specifically if you have a number of VIPs to accommodate.

get the pecking order right

Normally a hotel will quote a conference room rate, whereby you are expected to use a range of different types of room, subject to usage of the hotel by other guests. However, you are likely to have specific groups of delegates who need to be treated in a particular way. VIPs could include the CEO, top executives, celebrity speakers, major sponsors, famous entertainers and important guests from other organizations. Often the hotel conference manager will put the conference organizer in an upgraded room, as well as some of the organizing team, depending on room availability. When it comes to the delegates, you must opt for uniformity for people on the same grade. Conferences are often perceived by delegates as a reward – indeed, sometimes attendance is restricted to the upper echelons of the organization. For that reason, you need to ensure that, if there is a pecking order of status, it should be respected. If status is irrelevant, ensure that everyone is allocated the same standard of room. Double rooms are normal (even if for single occupancy). There are very few single rooms of a high standard in conference hotels, and on investigation you may find that single rooms contain a lower standard of facilities (shower cubicle instead of bath, for example) than you might expect, having seen the double-room equivalent.

rooming list

Having agreed your requirement for VIP rooms and indicated whether single or twin rooms are going to be acceptable, you will need to provide the hotel with an alphabetical rooming list, by delegate surname, with specific requirements marked (VIP, doubles). Allow the hotel some flexibility beyond this, otherwise they may struggle to match their space availability to your needs, especially if you are taking up virtually the whole hotel. Exclusivity of the hotel property is a good idea for incentive groups but not for conferences: it restricts your ability to vary the room repartition or total numbers as no-shows or last-minute acceptances are common.

Having arrived at the property the night before, you will need to check the room repartition plan so that you can make any last-minute adjustments. However, you must always bear in mind that, until the previous night's occupant has moved out (say by 11 am) and the room has been cleaned (say by 1.30 pm), your guest will not be able to check-in, so be very clear, both in your delegate instructions and in your arrangements with the hotel, what the official check-in time is. Avoid promising something you cannot deliver. You will need several copies of the rooming list for your organizing team and any senior executive who may want to contact some of the delegates quickly when they arrive at the conference.

trading off

A good hotel will always view the accommodation element of the conference as part of the whole project, which will include conference room hire and any on-site banqueting. If you are too demanding in terms of upgraded rooms and additional facilities for your delegates' overnight stay, you may find the hotel is less flexible on banqueting costs. There is always a trade-off between conference, banqueting and accommodation revenue in the eyes of the hotel, so take your concessions with good grace as you go through the process. The more business you can give the hotel (by opting to have the conference dinner on-site rather than off-site, for example), the better your rate or added value, particularly if your delegate numbers grow the nearer you get to conference day. Conversely, do not expect to retain any earlier concessions if your numbers fall substantially. The hotel will take a view, often a subjective one, and may well decide not to enforce their cancellation terms if you have been amenable in your dealings with them thus far, or can promise them more events at some future date.

your conference checklist

- ▦ Check your production and delegate needs together. ☐
- ▦ Ensure that you recognize the different room types. ☐
- ▦ Confirm your delegate rooming list. ☐
- ▦ Be flexible and trade-off to get the best deal. ☐

food and drink

No single element of a conference organizer's job has the potential to cause more problems than 'banqueting'. A hungry audience is a dangerous audience. Hunger makes people irritable, inattentive and likely to leave early. Times of eating and drinking may also be the delegates' only opportunity to socialize and swap gossip – a vital ingredient of any successful conference. Unfortunately too few organizers pay sufficient attention to the banqueting part of the conference programme, resulting in unhappy delegates and a poorly communicated corporate message.

what is banqueting?

What do we mean by banqueting? It can include the provision of tea, coffee and biscuits. It will undoubtedly involve the mid-conference luncheon arrangements. Banqueting is often erroneously taken to mean just the dinner before or after the conference. If your delegates are staying overnight, banqueting also means providing bar service, room service and breakfast. In some venues it can involve setting up restaurant facilities on a beach, in the desert or on top of a mountain. Banqueting staff are also responsible for the layout of rooms for functions, and for creating the right ambience to suit each occasion.

types of banqueting service

One potential area of confusion for the inexperienced conference organizer is what type of service to choose on each banqueting occasion. Buffet service? Plated starter? Silver service? Cash bar? Drinks at the table? Meal vouchers? Trayed cocktails? Open bar? Each situation is different, but clear instructions should be given to the banqueting or food and beverage (F & B) manager to avoid disgruntled delegates or a bar bill of horrendous proportions. Some knowledge of the various food-preparation systems currently used by the catering trade may be of value.

delivering a plated main course

For medium and large conferences, most of the food is prepared well in advance and arranged in such a way as to ease distribution. Modern hotels are designed so that final preparation areas are next to the banqueting rooms (if they are not, you may legitimately ask how they are going to serve the food and keep it hot in transit). Heated plates are essential, as are specialized refrigeration units for cold dishes. The various elements of the dish are added to the plate in rotation on a conveyor-belt, and the completed plates are placed in a mobile cart ready for waitress/waiter distribution. To serve 300 covers, with five employees, takes around 45 minutes.

Portion control is assured by using specific tools (ladles, slicers, scoops, etc) to make each plate look similar. This also helps to prevent overzealous catering staff from loading the plate too heavily and incurring complaints from neighbours of the overloaded diner.

Some choices of courses can cause specific preparation and

heating problems for large groups (soufflés, veal cutlets, flam-béed desserts) – so if there is a late change of choice, the chef needs to be involved so that his team can actually deliver the product. What you sampled at your inspection may not be at all suitable for 300 delegates, in preparation and distribution terms. For example, changing from chicken to duck on the morning of the evening gala dinner may simply not be possible, for two reasons. First, the chef may not be able to acquire a large quantity of duck so quickly, and secondly, even if he can, it is likely to come frozen and will need to be defrosted before it can be cooked. It is always wise to follow the menu choices offered by the venue, as these will have been tried and tested with many previous customers and amended if they have proved difficult to deliver in practice.

choosing the menus

Anyone can choose from a menu, but the two- or three-day conference organizer needs to bear in mind who the delegates are, what they ate yesterday or even the day before, and what they are going to eat tomorrow. You will also need to take into account any activities they may be undertaking as part of the conference programme, and choose accordingly.

breakfast

Breakfast is relatively easy to deal with, as few delegates would object to the same choice of breakfast each day, unlike lunch or dinner. However, recent trends in healthy eating mean less meats and fat and more fresh fruit and skimmed milk. If the conference is also part incentive, exotic fruit dishes, special teas and coffees or themed buffets are not unusual. A buffet-style breakfast, where guests help themselves at designated points, has become the most popular service method the world over. It also saves on the hotel's labour costs and creates the circumstances for rapid turnaround of delegates – often essential if the conference is to start on time.

You need to consider opting for a private breakfast buffet, rather than allowing delegates to drift down to the main breakfast area with other guests. Hotels have an acute operational feel for how individual business guests will behave over the two- or three-hour breakfast gap, and they gear up their service accordingly. But conference delegates do not behave normally. They cluster about 45 minutes before the conference starts, and need serving instantly. For that reason having a private function facility is better than relying on the normal breakfast room being able to cope, however reassuring the hotel may be during the site visit.

luncheon

By definition, luncheon is squeezed between the morning and the afternoon sessions. It therefore has a very defined time constraint which the caterers need to work around.

Most delegates would say that a buffet-style service would produce a quicker throughput (it does for breakfast, so why not for lunch?). However, in practice, a plated sit-down luncheon is far easier to control in terms of time. Appetisers or first courses can be pre-plated and placed at the table settings, ready for when delegates break from the morning session. Vegetables and sauces can be placed centrally on each table, with only the entrées being distributed from heated trays at the appropriate moment. Dessert can be cold (fruit, ice-cream) so that the timing of bringing them up from the kitchens is less crucial. If price is an issue, portion control is less easy with a buffet and the cost to the conference organizer tends to be higher.

In terms of food choice, if the main purpose of the event is the conference not the luncheon, you need to choose light dishes so as not to put the delegates to sleep. Heavy sauces, rich desserts, red meat, all conspire to immobilize the delegate, both physically and mentally. Most organizers tend to opt for fish or chicken dishes, followed by a fruit-based dessert, to ensure an attentive afternoon audience.

dinner

But dinner is a different matter. Usually, you want your delegates to relax and take their time, so the menu choice can be a little more relaxed. Most conference venues will have a pre-printed choice of starters, main courses and desserts. The London Marriott, for example, offers a choice of 10 appetizers, 10 main courses and 10 desserts, which you can mix and match for the same price. Other hotels offer a graded choice depending upon the cost of the ingredients used. Although you are perfectly entitled to choose what you want, take advice from the food and beverage manager who will be thinking both about the balance of the meal and the hotel's ability to deliver it to a uniform standard for all the delegates. Bear in mind that although pork and veal appear in almost every important conference venue's menu options, the average delegate can be quite conservative. Fish as a main course can be a problem for a significant minority, so you choose it at your peril for a main course at a gala dinner. (You can always add a fourth meat course if you want to hedge your bets.) Be aware that, although themed banquets may seem like a good, creative idea, a complete Chinese meal to support next year's Hong Kong incentive may not be popular if there is no alternative. One course in theme (such as the starter) can serve the same purpose and have the desired creative touch without alienating all those who prefer standard fare.

Special diets need special care. You should know who needs what special diet from your pre-event questionnaire. At meal-times, these individuals need to be highlighted to waiting staff so that the relevant alternative dish gets to the right person. It is always worth checking personally with the special-diet delegate whether they realize what is on the menu, as they may suddenly and inexplicably change their mind. Conversely, you need to dissuade or politely disallow other delegates from suddenly becoming 'special diet' when they see the alternative, otherwise there will be serious kitchen delays as the chef tries to cope with creating alternative meals from scratch – not to mention the waste of the pre-ordered courses.

Food is a very personal thing. But it is the conference organizer's job to steer a diplomatic path between creating an attractive menu and being able to deliver it at the right temperature to a large number of people to the same high standard. Take advice from the catering professionals, whose job it is to deliver large quantities of quality meals every day of their lives, and you will not go far wrong. Be wary of delegating menu choices to the CEO's wife or 'someone who likes cooking' in your organization. Like every other conference-organizing task, planning and making informed choices is what good banqueting is all about.

booking the right function room

As you know from reading Chapter 6 ('Accommodating your conference'), altering the layout of a room can make a big difference to delegate capacity. However, the key issue for a venue banqueting manager is the yield per room in terms of food and beverage. All venues are aware of the profit generation from each function room they manage, and will be reluctant to place the wrong size of group in a particular room because it may mean that they have to turn away a more profitable group at some later stage. Having said that, if you think that the ambience and creative style of holding a dinner for 20 people in a room that could accommodate 100 is worth paying for, go ahead – but do not be surprised if you are asked to pay a premium for the privilege. The closer you are to the event, the less likely it is that the venue will find an alternative client for a particular room, so if large room/small number of diners is your game plan, wait until the last minute before asking to switch and you could get a bargain.

Whatever approach you take, you need to satisfy yourself that you know the answers to the following questions.

■ Is there enough space for the cabaret entertainment and/or portable bar, as well as the delegates?
■ Will delegates need to be seated or could they stand (you need about one square metre, or 10 square feet, per delegate if seated, about 0.8 square metres, 9 square feet, if they stand)?
■ Is the room easily accessible for both staff and delegates?
■ Check the sizes of tables and chairs to be used. A slight increase on standard dimensions could reduce delegate capacity significantly.
■ What will be going on in the adjacent function room? If it is a disco, will this spoil your CEO's after-dinner speech?
■ If the room is completely or partially outdoors, what is the wet weather back-up (and the access to that alternative for both delegates and staff)?

When you book the room (or more usually several rooms), do so in writing and specify timings and the types of function envisaged, together with any information regarding special decoration, cabaret or musical entertainment. Decisions about the size of room should not be taken solely on the basis of delegate invitees. If numbers are difficult to quantify, start with the maximum and option smaller rooms too, just in case your confirmed numbers dwindle. It is better to be up-front with the venue from the outset, as they may be considering the logistics of simultaneously handling groups from other clients and will be better placed than you to make sensible decisions about which rooms to use.

drink and be merry

An important part of every conference meal is the management of beverages, but this need not always involve alcohol. As with the organization of the food options, both you, as conference organizer, and the venue should be clear what the policy is on beverages well before the delegates arrive.

beverage events

Beverage events include:

- breakfast;
- tea and coffee breaks;
- pre-lunch drinks;
- luncheon;
- cocktail reception;
- dinner;
- bar.

Each of these events can be classified as either hosted (where the sponsor pays) or non-hosted (where the delegate pays). Much will depend on the type of event you are running and its history as to which ones are hosted and which ones are non-hosted. But make sure that the food and beverage manager and your delegates know which is which.

breakfast

In a conference context, as far as beverages are concerned, breakfast suffers from the same problems as meal service.

Invariably a significant minority of delegates rises early only to find the breakfast arrangements may not be ready at the stated time or are poorly serviced. In particular, items such as decaffeinated coffee or a range of fruit juices need to be specified in advance, otherwise the first you hear of dissatisfaction is in the post-event analysis.

As the conference organizer, you need to be awake and alert before breakfast-time in order to check on the delivery of what has been agreed. You only need one early riser to infect the rest of the group with tales of bad service or inflexible catering. Conferences are not an occasion to catch up on your own sleep quota.

breaks

Tea or coffee intervals either side of luncheon (or indeed at registration) must be treated as an integral part of the conference programme, rather than an irritating, physiological interlude. If it is an upbeat conference with good news to impart, perhaps related to an incentive, you may decide that some theming may be appropriate.

If the purpose of the conference is to forge bonding of some sort between the delegates, serving the break beverages within the same room is less effective than having a separate room with a different atmosphere, where delegates can choose to talk about social things rather than the business of the day. Privacy is essential to create the group feeling, so corridors and public areas are not a good idea. A smattering of chairs and tables helps to encourage small informal groups of five or six, which can lead to broader subjects of conversation than one-to-one chats.

We have talked about the logistical elements of having a short break and many people to serve. From a beverages point of view, you need to have adequate supplies prepared beforehand (4.5 litres, or one gallon, make 20 coffees), because by the time you have brewed up more the break will be over. One trick is to move the condiments to other tables to reduce the effect of queuing at the beverage dispenser; you could also place dispensers at the far end of the room to draw delegates through the available hospitality area.

time of day

Breaks run during the afternoon should include iced water and soft drinks. Research shows that, given a choice, almost two-thirds of delegates will opt for soft drinks or water rather than tea or coffee during the afternoon, although this does depend on the dominant nationality. Alcoholic drinks will make delegates sleepy. If such a state is desired, perhaps with an incentive group, go ahead. Otherwise be aware that alcohol makes for a less attentive audience.

The valedictory break, before delegates leave for home, needs careful consideration. If they are mostly driving home it would be irresponsible, as well as unwise, to provide alcohol. If they are staying overnight as your guests, then celebratory cocktails after a hard day's work are good hospitality and can only serve to enhance the efforts of the day's communications activities and objectives.

drinks before or during luncheon

Many a sound corporate communications plan has been ruined by the injudicious provision of alcohol before and during luncheon. The golden rule is that, if you want delegates to sit up and take notice during the post-lunch 'graveyard' session of the conference, do not serve alcohol. Nothing is more guaranteed to provide mass somnolence than copious amounts of wine.

One way around this is to balance the alcohol (white wine)

with a light lunch (fish or chicken) and a 'healthy' dessert (pineapple), deliberately opting not to refill glasses and providing plenty of bottled water. But in recent years, the trend towards alcohol-free lunches has been marked, particularly for one-day conferences, so do not feel obliged to offer it. Be reassured that these days fewer and fewer sponsors provide it, unless they intend deliberately to generate bonhomie. A leading survey by venue-search specialists Banks Sadler revealed that the proportion of organizers placing restrictions on lunch-time alcohol had risen from 47 per cent to 62 per cent in recent years.

gala dinner drinking

Apocryphal stories abound when it comes to recounting the excesses of the conference gala dinner. These range from mild inebriation to mass arrests and the razing to the ground of the chosen venue. Much can be laid at the door of an inappropriate or inexperienced beverages policy.

On the one hand, part of your job as 'party organizer' is to ensure that everyone has a good time. Conversely, you need to stay within budget and avoid the organizational consequences of excessive drunkenness and disorder.

You can opt to pay by the drink (a flat fee per person) or by the bottle. Paying for each drink (coke, double brandy, vodka tonic, malt whisky) can prove expensive if the delegates have exotic tastes. A flat fee per delegate, based on an agreed range of alcohol to be offered, works out cheaper. This is the method often used for cocktail parties, where a specific time limit usually operates and consumption can be easily estimated. The most usual method of payment for wine at a gala dinner is by the bottle. However, the system is open to abuse. Some unscrupulous venues often make 'mistakes' when counting up the empty bottles. Or they deliberately uncork many more bottles than you need and insist that you pay for them, whether or not they have been used.

You need to be alert to these practices and establish before the event begins what you will pay for and what you will not. Insistence on personally signing any chits for drinks above budget is a good discipline.

bar service

The bar service which often follows the gala dinner needs to be equally well regulated. Whether you have an open bar at the sponsors' expense or a cash bar, you need to check the prices to be charged and have a specific policy for overspend authorization or time limit. Often you may wish to authorize certain senior individuals to have the facility to charge drinks to the house account. You should make it clear to the bar staff that you will only pay for drinks invoices bearing the relevant, agreed signatures.

It is difficult to be accurate about consumption as each group is different. But it is generally true that men drink more than women, that more white wine than red is drunk at gala dinners (usually in the ratio 3:1) and that the provision of water greatly reduces wine intake and the general level of inebriation. If you are calculating how many bottles you may need, there are six glasses of wine per bottle and, depending on the amount of entertainment available, you could expect people to drink 2.5 glasses per hour for the first hour and one per hour thereafter. But like all these ratios, your group is likely to be the exception. They key point is that you should be in regular contact with the food and beverage manager or designated head waiter, and keep up-to-date on where you are when it comes to hosted consumption.

nightcap

The bar arrangements often go awry when the official function is over and the core of hard drinkers settles in for the night (and often well into the morning). As in all other banqueting aspects, decide a policy, brief the staff and make it clear what your expectations are. It is to be hosted or non-hosted? Should the bar close at 1 am to 2 am? What evidence do you require of bottles opened or drinks served? What are the approved signatures? If you have clearly communicated on these issues, the only people with a headache the next morning will be those who stayed up late to drink the bar dry.

summary

The food and drink aspects of a conference are an essential ingredient of its success. Because they represent a considerable proportion of the budget, they need to be chosen wisely and carefully monitored.

your conference checklist

- ▧ Choose menus which can be delivered. ☐
- ▧ Book the right size of function room. ☐
- ▧ Establish a beverages policy. ☐
- ▧ Ensure that the venue knows who are the authorized signatories for extra drinks. ☐

going abroad

It is tempting to think that organizing a conference abroad is the same as doing it in your own country, with the added element of an international flight. To some extent, it is. In essence, you have a long list of items to coordinate and organize into the most effective time sequence. But the biggest difference is lack of control. Because the language and culture may be different and the preparation time spent at the venue is often restricted, you need a specialist team of assistants to facilitate the process and minimize potential errors. You can do it all yourself, of course – but you will not accomplish much else back in your office if you are head cook and bottle washer for a major overseas event. Few conference organizers have the luxury of only having one event to run at any one time, so it is vital to pick the right partners if you are going to keep your head above water and deliver the standard expected by your organization for an overseas event.

partners to consider

Depending on your degree of experience and the resources within your organization, you may wish to choose from one or more of the following suppliers:

▨ travel agent or business travel house;
▨ local ground agent or DMC (destination management company);
▨ production agency with international experience;
▨ overseas conference management specialists.

The pros and cons of each of these will now be assessed.

travel agent

Because of the cross-border complexities of organizing third-party travel for independent delegates from various parts of the globe, conference delegates normally make their own way to the venue and pay for the travel themselves. However, if yours is a staff conference for which the organization will eventually settle the travel bill, you need to take on the task, with your travel supplier, of advising and booking delegates on to suitable means of transport. As time is precious in any business, this usually means flights. Ways to save costs include booking all the seats through one or two well-connected air carriers rather than allowing a free-for-all. If you can get your delegates to travel in groups of 10 or more, group discounts may apply. A further advantage of controlling the flights is that you, as conference organizer, know who is supposed to be arriving when. This means that you can organize airport transfers at the appropriate time and act quickly in the case of delays. If you do not know when delegates are due to arrive, how will you know whether to start your conference on time? They could be five minutes late or five hours late. Again, economies of size will mean that you can lay on larger transfer buses at a less expensive pre-head price than that of reimbursing individual taxi fares. Knowing where the delegates have to return to can also impinge on your programme planning. If there is a significant contingent returning to the other side of the world on the 6 pm flight it would be insensitive to plan a programme that finishes too late for them to catch their plane (not to mention the extra expense of an additional overnight stay).

destination management companies

Destination management companies (DMCs) or ground agents exist in most conference destinations. Usually small, with a staple business in package-tour clients and individual business travellers, DMCs provide transfers, tours and out-of-hotel hospitality ideas to augment your programme. You cannot be everywhere, so you need a team of people with local knowledge to pick up your incoming delegates at the airport, deliver them to the hotel or conference centre, organize any local tours and manage specific non-venue events. Only rarely will you get the chance to see for yourself how a banqueting venue might cope with the group of your particular size or profile. The DMC, if they are any good, will narrow down the options, walk you through the logistics on a site inspection and reassure you with past case-histories of how the venue works in practice. It could be an out-of-town country estate, a wine cellar, a dine-around (a series of small, local restaurants) or a spectacular staged event in a castle. Whatever it is, you need locals with contacts who can make things happen and provide the appropriate level of service.

You simply cannot choose a restaurant for 100 delegates on the basis of your own or the CEO's private visit there six months earlier. Often, foreign restaurateurs will not take bookings direct, as they value the role of a local DMC too highly and do not need the hassle of a foreign client who might not turn up – or, worse still, not pay up. This is particularly true in Mediterranean countries, where personal contacts and relationships still mean a lot.

production agency

In Chapter 4 we looked at the services that a professional

production company can offer in order to create a successful conference in the UK. To do the same job overseas requires an extra dimension of know-how. The show itself may be identical, but getting the equipment to the venue, setting it up, de-rigging it and bringing it all home again through international borders requires a mountain of paperwork and a thorough knowledge of certain bureaucratic regimes around the world.

Although regulations do change, your production company will invariably need to draw up a complete list of technical equipment so that it can be 'exported'. It also needs to 'import' exactly the same list of items when it returns, otherwise all the equipment can be impounded indefinitely. In some parts of the world all may be in order – but they will need to provide a 'gift' to the customs official in order to have the equipment waved through. Stories are legion of essential computer hardware being held up in customs warehouses pending a bureaucrat's stamp.

On arrival at the venue, unless the technical crew have done their homework thoroughly, you could find inadequate power sources, incompatible systems and a general lack of spare parts and back-up equipment. Part of your checking process with a production company should be to ask what duplicate equipment they intend to take, in case of failure, and what bureaucratic or technical problems they anticipate in the chosen country of the planned event.

You cannot afford to allow the presentation element to go wrong, especially as every conference is 'live' and you cannot rerun it in the event of technical difficulties. Ask for previous case histories, query the administrative processes used to get equipment in and out of foreign countries, and, above all, check the contingencies for equipment failure or customs delays. Cheapest is not always best when it comes to running productions and presentation events overseas.

overseas conference management specialists

If you opt to appoint an overseas conference management specialist, you need to be very clear about lines of responsibility. Decide who should run the delegate travel elements, who should deal with the hotel, who should deal with the off-site issues and who should produce the show. It may be that one company can undertake all these elements on a project-fee basis. In other circumstances, you may wish to handle the conference production company yourself so that you can concentrate on what the delegate experiences in terms of the corporate message.

If you appoint more than one outside specialist, encourage them to liaise directly so that last-minute glitches can be smoothed over without necessarily involving you. They may also be able to see some cost-saving opportunities. If the logistics company were able to get a special group-rate for the travel, this could be passed on to the production crew when they travel out a few days before. Or the hotel may want to buy the stage set for another client rather than have it de-rigged, which you may not have known if it were not for the relationship between the local DMC and the hotel's management.

destination options

Choosing an overseas conference venue is not like choosing a holiday. You need to consider the facilities of the venue for the type of conference you intend to run, and the international access for your delegate profile.

Table 8.1 shows a rank order of conference destinations, measured by their instant appeal, as perceived by European conference organizers. Some of these places score low because of poor marketing or cultural issues, but almost all are characterized by good access and have significant conference facilities compared to other world cities.

Choice of venue is as much about fashion and taste as it is about price and accessibility. Athens lost its way a little in the 1990s and is trying to recover by upgrading its conference infrastructure. Zurich or Geneva may seem to be disproportionately high on the list, given the global scope of the survey, but excellent air access and good facilities have meant that organizations use these places time and time again because they work well.

Table 8.1   Appeal of conference destinations

Destination	Average score (out of 10)	Destination	Average score (out of 10)
Paris	8.0	Los Angeles	6.4
Hawaii	7.8	Lisbon	6.4
Hong Kong	7.5	Budapest	6.3
Singapore	7.5	Brussels	6.3
New York	7.5	Edinburgh	6.2
Geneva	7.4	Copenhagen	6.1
London	7.4	Milan	5.9
Cannes	7.3	Stockholm	5.9
Monaco	7.3	Istanbul	5.8
Rome	7.1	Cyprus	5.8
Florence	7.1	Munich	5.8
Nice	7.1	Frankfurt	5.7
Vienna	7.0	Athens	5.6
Amsterdam	6.9	Dublin	5.6
Bangkok	6.8	Luxembourg	5.3
Barcelona	6.7	Marbella	5.3
Berlin	6.7	Helsinki	5.2
Madrid	6.4	Cairo	4.9
Miami	6.4	Dubai	4.3
Zurich	6.4	Glasgow	4.2

By kind permission: Reed Publishing

communication

If you are not using an international event management agency, you must pay serious attention to communicating with the venue. Terminology differences around the world can lead to significant errors (eg suite, twin, breakdown, attrition, rack rate), especially when it comes to settling the bill. You need to keep on top of the file and ask for clarification if there is anything you do not understand. Just like at home, a venue may neglect to tell you about roadworks outside the main entrance or a religious festival that means that no alcohol can be served for 24 hours. Do not assume that, because some venue services or local taxes are included in the UK, they are included in the USA or the UAE. If in doubt, ask.

currency

Most overseas conferences end up costing more than envisaged at the outset through nobody's fault, due to currency movements. You could find that, in certain parts of the world, up to 80 per cent of your budget must be paid in a foreign currency or in US dollars. It can be well worth your while asking your finance department whether they want to buy forward to protect against an adverse movement in the currency of the bill to be paid.

Some international organizations may not find it possible to move profits across borders, so one reason for holding a cross-border conference in a particular country could be to use surplus cash which would otherwise be frozen. This is particularly true in the newly emerging eastern European countries or the Far East.

language and culture

With an overseas conference, interpreting and translation issues are not just limited to the conference room. They start with the initial invitation and need to be considered when dele-gates are picked up at the airport or given a cultural tour. Never assume that the language of convenience is always English.

During social events such as cocktail parties and off-site dining, you will need to think through the potential culture clash between the host country and your mix of delegates. Public drinking is frowned upon in Beijing, access to certain public buildings can be tricky in St Petersburg, and women in short skirts and sleeveless tops do not go down well in Muslim countries. Eating times may be dramatically different. Dinner at 6 pm in Los Angeles is normal, whereas in Madrid you would not expect to sit down to an evening meal before 10 pm – and even that is a bit early for most Madrilenos.

but why bother to go abroad at all?

The most powerful incentive you can offer people is the oppor-tunity to travel overseas. Travel works as a motivator. If you need to attract a certain type of delegate, or simply to say thank you for a job well done within the framework of a conference, going overseas makes good commercial sense. But it creates a new dimension of challenges for the conference organizer which affects every aspect of the organizational plan. As with other marketing communications issues, get the right level of advice and take it, especially if the people you are using have been there before. The last thing you should be doing is using your delegates as pioneers in an uncertain world.

your conference checklist

▨ Choose your overseas partners carefully. ☐
▨ Assess your destinations options. ☐
▨ Think about currency movements. ☐
▨ Consider potential culture clashes. ☐

what went right, what went wrong

After any marketing activity such as a conference, you should do some research. In essence you need to ask the delegates what they thought – but you should also extend this procedure to suppliers and ask them how they think it went. Why? Because the findings create the perfect blueprint for how to improve your next conference. No one ever gets it right first time round. A little humility is a good principle if you are genuinely interested in making your next conference even better.

Where to start? Unless something went disastrously wrong and no one can agree why, or you have organized a very large event, the research does not necessarily need to be handled by an independent research agency. You can do it yourself. But you do need to be aware of the principles of a good research process, otherwise the answers you get may not be of great use.

carrying out the research

The research process can be broken down into eight stages, from conception to completion:

1. Identify the item (our conference, or an issue within the whole event);
2. Create the research design;
3. Choose the research methodology (telephone, letter, e-mail);
4. Select the sample(s)
5. Collect the data (at the conference or afterwards);
6. Analyse the data;
7. Present the data (to the budget sponsors);
8. Follow-up (with an action plan).

In addition, anonymity of the respondents helps to boost response and create the environment for more honest answers. Proximity (in time) to the event will solicit more accurate replies. I would defy anyone to rate the standard of banqueting service five or six weeks after an event.

Bearing these stages in mind, you then need to construct a suitable methodology and questionnaire for your conference delegates.

methodology

You have a choice of how to get the answers you need:

■ at the event;
■ after the event, by mail;
■ after the event, by telephone;
■ by group discussion or individual interview.

Some organizers favour a pre-printed questionnaire, which delegates complete as the event is in progress. If you are researching speaker style and content, this is almost essential. However, you do need to be aware that an overall view of the event will be impossible to gauge until the end, so comparative comments about early-day sessions may be less valuable, as they will not have been assessed in the context of the other sessions which followed.

Distributing questionnaires to delegates as they leave the conference is another option. Using this method, the replies may be more considered – the delegates will have had time to think about the event in its entirety and be able to make better overall judgements. (They can also provide some feedback about how the return travel logistics were handled, if relevant.) The number of returned questionnaires is likely to be quite low though, and so the results may not be representative.

A better method is to follow up a statistically relevant sample by telephone within a couple of days of the conference. For a group of 100, you may need to make 25 calls. For a group of 500, 75 would do. If anonymity is guaranteed, you will get a more honest view. Delegates can be taken through a series of questions for up to 30 minutes if required, as they are often keen to provide a critique. But aim for 15 minutes so as not to appear to be taking up their time with an unproductive (in their eyes) activity.

If it is absolutely vital to get to the bottom of a particular issue, or if there is some general disagreement about 'what went wrong', a group discussion conducted by a professional research agency or facilitator may be the only way. With this technique you are looking for quality, not statistical accuracy. The discussions will help to bring the real issues to the surface; these could then be checked by mail or telephone canvass to gauge the seriousness of the particular issue. However, in the vast majority of cases you are probably hoping to discover minor improvements to the process for the future, if you have done your job properly.

Supplier research should take place in the form of a debriefing session with both sides saying what went well and what went less well. This is an invaluable way to improve the future working relationship, as each side gains a clearer understanding of the other's expectations.

Research important items only

The aim of all good research should be to ask meaningful questions. It would be nice to know, for example, whether the delegates thought their seats were comfortable – but it is probably not as essential as other issues, like the rating of speakers' content.

Some topics to concentrate on for any event would be:

	Score (From 1, poor, to 5, excellent)
▓ Achievement of original objectives	☐
▓ Speaker delivery/style	☐
▓ Speaker content/relevance	☐
▓ Quality of staging	☐
▓ Pre-event communication	☐
▓ Travel arrangements	☐
▓ Registration	☐
▓ Organization of breaks	☐
▓ Organization and standard of luncheon	☐
▓ Overall balance of the conference programme	☐
▓ Gala dinner	☐
▓ Overnight arrangements	☐
▓ Value of the conference to delegates	☐

It is worth remembering that you may have had an excellent speaker, but the content might have been irrelevant for that particular audience. For speaker evaluations, you may wish to separate style and professionalism from content. Try to avoid loading the questions in your favour as organizer, otherwise the exercise becomes devalued. Closed questions ('Please rate on a scale...') are better than open questions ('What did you think of...'), as open questions can lead to answers that defy categorization and so are open to the interpretation of the statistical compiler.

presenting the findings

Presentation of the findings needs some thought. Even if you have 50 pages of answers, not everyone will want to wade through them all. Some of the answers may only be of relevance to you. Home in on the known key issues, and support your findings with statistics and a typical quotation for each result.

Here is an extract from a real event, which took place at a resort hotel on the south coast of the UK, with an international group of 100 senior managers. It combined a standard conference with learning how to sail a 19th-century square-rigged sailing ship. The names have been changed to protect the innocent (or guilty).

conference research example

1 General comments

- The weakest elements of the event overall were the outside speakers (with the exception of speaker A) – with speaker B and speaker C rated of 'lowest' value. However, all the speakers had their fans as well as their critics!
- Speaker A was rated as one of the 'highest' elements of the event (perhaps indicating that the delegates respond better to speakers of greater 'celebrity' status who are known internationally!).
- The hotel was rated highly, both as an event venue and for standard of catering, falling down slightly on accommodation standards. However, there were a number of comments about the general impression of decline at the hotel and questioning of the 5-star rating!
- The sailing concept was the single most highly rated factor, receiving only high to excellent ratings, the vast majority being 'excellent'.

- The second most highly rated factor was the service from the administration team.
- Other items which received a significant 'high' rating were the event documentation – although interestingly several delegates did not give this item a rating and others commented that they did not consider this an important/significant factor!

2 Breakdown of comments

Positives	Negatives	Future reference
Successful event which was well planned/organized and executed. (Much better than last year – no comparison!)	Programme balance – either cut down sailing or extend event to include more business sessions.	More business focus – particularly on strategy objectives, developments in each stream.
Concept was different, bold, radical and worked.	More time should have been spent on group strategy issues.	Highlight significant/ exemplary developments in each stream.
'Activity' content enhanced the success while providing an excellent and stimulating vehicle for team-building and interaction.	SWOT sessions should have been longer (up to 1 day).	More input from 'internal' speakers, eg Main Board, New Acquisitions, Management
Provided a unique opportunity to work together towards a common goal and as a result strengthened team relations.	Objectives too ambitious/event did not lend itself to achieving all objectives. Less in more depth would have been better.	Stream events alternate years.

Positives	Negatives	Future reference
▓ Provided good opportunity for networking with colleagues and new contacts.	▓ More leisure/free time for informal networking.	▓ Events held more frequently – minimum every 2 years.
▓ The analogies between business/ sailing added to the impact (including theme and title).	▓ Outside speakers did not 'add value'. They had nothing 'new' to say.	▓ Venue more accessible/improve on standard.

In this example, percentages were less important than the overall findings, but you could deduce from these comments that next time the company runs a similar conference, they will certainly think more carefully about using outside speakers and spend more time debating the strategy of the business.

taking action

The post-event report (including any objective research) is only as good as the action you take as a result of it. Some findings may indicate minor logistical improvements ('include a map') which, taken together as a package of small measures, will help to improve hygiene and convenience issues. However, the real value of post-event research is to uncover any major discrepancies between what was offered and the delegates' expectations. Whether it is an internal event or one which delegates pay to attend, a meticulously organized conference is no good if the platform content is wrong. Only unbiased research from the audience will tell you where you went wrong and how to avoid doing it next time.

Research can also help with budget planning. Often the expenditure on staging elements means there is precious little left over for 'front of house'. If you think this is an issue, skewing your research to cover the importance of hiring well-known speakers, a big-name cabaret ariste, having spectacular presentation effects or post-event video souvenirs, can help to isolate major expense items. This could lead you to conclude that spending more on accommodation and banqueting, and less on staging, would be a more effective use of the available budget, leading to a more successful conference next time.

garbage in, garbage out

As with all research, you need to ensure that you are clear as to what you hope to discover from the research. A report which merely supports your own predetermined view is of no use to you or your organization. Take time to frame the questions as objectively as you can so that you get as unbiased a view as possible. If there have been errors, it is in your interest more than anyone else's to get them put right in time for your next event.

your conference checklist

- ▨ Prepare the stages of the research process. ☐
- ▨ Decide your methodology. ☐
- ▨ Be objective and preserve anonymity. ☐
- ▨ Take action on the results. ☐

the future of conferences

The conference industry has already embraced the future with open arms. It can provide live voting on speaker issues, instant electronic transcripts of what speakers are saying or register delegates by a swipe of their name badge. If it is possible, conference organizers are willing to try it. But delegates are not so far behind. The audience is now almost as comfortable with new technology as the people organizing the event.

Each new business-to-business survey brings with it even more startling evidence about how many ordinary people are now connected to the Internet, using e-mail and downloading essential information from Web sites. It is clear that the average conference delegate is becoming more and more computer-literate. The need to travel up and down the country, or even from country to country, to collect information or to be briefed face-to-face on corporate issues is becoming a thing of the past. In the same way that e-mail has all but done away with the well-timed paper memo arriving in your in-tray, it could be argued that new technology is doing away with the need to meet with others in person. The days of the local or national conference seem to be numbered.

If we assume that many of today's conferences are still held mainly to impart information, the future for both conferences and conference organizers is going to be somewhat different. There are a number of new, but largely under-promoted, electronic services to facilitate the distribution of information that simply did not exist even five years ago. With the advent of WAP (wireless application protocol), which allows users to gather information without a telephone line, and pressure on Internet service providers to reduce their charges or provide them for free, we may well be at the beginning of a whole new way of doing business. This will undoubtedly change the reasons for holding a conference in the first place and, by implication, the job of the conference organizer.

CTI, ISDN and ADSL

The big difference that now makes *not* meeting up a distinct possibility is CTI (computer telephony integration).The use of telephone lines to transmit information other than voice has transformed the traditional cascade of information through organizations and between suppliers and buyers. But it was not until recently that this technological advance could be used to full advantage. The cabling that telephone companies used was simply not up to the job. Data would get lost in transit or, if it was images, the end result for the receiver was a bitty, grainy and slow-moving picture, which was often difficult to decipher.

Now, with ISDN (Integrated Services Digital Network), a much-improved carrying device for messages, large amounts of data and moving pictures are easily transported around the world. Using the recognized current standard for video-conferencing known as 'H320', seeing is believing. The screen picture you see now is as good as if you were in the same room.

The most recent technology is ADSL (Asymmetric Digital Subscriber Loop). In essence, it allows even more data to be transmitted at higher speeds than ISDN, enabling the problem of instant interaction to be largely solved. These days, not only can you see a 'live' image of the people you are conferencing with, you can interact directly in real time with gestures, pointers, electronic pencils and other devices to emphasize a particular point of view. All these improvements are being used to help individuals to communicate with other individuals across the business world.

video-conferencing

It goes without saying that the point of most business meetings is to discuss problems, change attitudes, express opinions and, sometimes, have your own mind changed about an issue or a product – sometimes by 180 degrees. But, by definition, conferences are group activities involving simultaneous interaction between many participants. Can this really be simulated electronically?

Hilton Hotels Corporation now offers video-conferencing for groups through its TeleSuite system. Rather than using separate monitors for each participant, the system uses a large, flat screen affixed to one of the conference-room walls, with a background that simulates the actual background of the room. This 'video mirror' creates the illusion that your 10 or so delegates are all in the same room. Any wires or technical equipment are hidden by strategically placed bowls of fruit or flowers, as are the microphones. With this technology, there arises the prospect of 'virtual breakfasts' – even 'tele-dining' is a reality now. You can actually have dinner with your client, even if you are on the other side of the world, without leaving your home town.

For smaller groups, the hardware and software now exists to cut down on the time taken to attend regular, low-level meetings. 3M markets the Advanced Meeting Solutions range, which uses video, audio, electronic whiteboard and data transfer products to enable participants to interact while staying in their own location. Such systems are particularly useful if the objective of the meeting is simply to agree a document and have a finished item available for distribution by the end of the meeting, eg a legal contract.

For larger groups, there are many types of virtual-conference software now available, facilitated by the Internet. With these systems, organizers announce the event online, giving details of the speakers, times and supporting data or graphics to be used. Participants then log on at home or their place of work and either read the presentations off the screen or listen through an audio link. Questions can be put live to the presenter, as in a chatroom, or recorded for future reply.

reducing the need to travel

Recent surveys of the cost of business travel show that up to 50 per cent of the time spent getting to and attending meetings in distant locations is wasted time. Business development or representation can now be done interactively using the Internet, CD-ROMs and the buyer's own PC. The product can now be demonstrated at a fraction of the cost of a site visit, and in a much more leisurely way. Some buyers may even prefer not to have a representative present, so that they can evaluate the product without pressure. Imparting information, the stuff of most conferences in the past, will be facilitated through more widespread use of the Internet, with browser links helping customers to search for what they need to know. Many international companies have already cut their business travel budgets substantially and are looking at more ways to make travelling unnecessary. Even major corporate decisions could be made through video-conferencing, which could be particularly important in fast-moving global businesses, where speed of reaction could mean winning more market share.

clear message

A secondary, but important, point about electronic communication is that it provides the potential for uniformity. Roadshows to launch new products are notorious for being too reliant on the local venue or presenter. If the message is controlled and is the same whenever and wherever it is relayed to the target audience, then marketing is more effective. For conference organizers, this could mean reducing presentation costs as the professional presenter may only need to be paid once, and the expense of the roadshow crew and other travel costs would disappear.

Other factors such as 'social loafing' can be mitigated. Behavioural scientists have proved that the more people there are in a group, the less effort each individual makes. In the context of a large conference it is easy for individuals, if they are so inclined, to relax and not take on board the essential messages the sponsor wishes to impart. With one-to-one communication, lack of attention is virtually eliminated as viewing can be tracked and, in some circumstances, knowledge can be tested after the broadcast is over by means of a distance-learning module.

conferences to change attitudes

We may not be too far from a time when there is very little point in holding a conference for large numbers of delegates simply to relay information, because data will be disseminated in a variety of other ways on personal communication systems. There will be no need to have a conference to exchange information.

Now the third millennium is here, we might legitimately ask ourselves how we should best communicate with large numbers of people if data can be sent so cheaply and easily around the world. There are still vast conference centres being built both by governments and commercial groups. What sort of conferences do they think they will attract in this new age of instant, reliable communication?

The future of conferences must surely lie in *how* they are used. Perhaps promoting attitude change, creating group loyalty and rewarding positive behaviour could be the answer. In the future, attending a conference will be an exciting occasion where the delegates expect to learn something they did not know, be converted to a new way of thinking about the sponsors' products or ideas or be rewarded for having done a good job. Concentrating on audience attitude changes and perceptions will be what conference organizers of the future will be paid to do. A successful conference will be one where the audience experiences a major shift in attitude, rather than collects vast amounts of corporate information. Listening to what the delegate is thinking and measuring what they learnt will become the key issues.

the human touch

It is always tempting to think in business that when the future comes, technology will replace all the normal processes involved in creating commercial value. Despite the exciting developments in information technology, there still remains a place for good, old-fashioned human contact and building relationships. The sparkle in the eye, the laughter of the audience and the feeling of belonging are difficult to replicate, whatever technology you choose to use. For the foreseeable future, there will still be benefits to meeting together as human beings to create better ways and improved processes.

Deciding what form conferences should take in the future is one of those issues that will not be resolved by the Internet alone. It will require the humn touch to make it work effectively. That will be the challenge for conference organizers of the future.